BOOKS BY ROBERT UNDERHILL

The Truman Persuasions
The Bully Pulpit
FDR and Harry: Parallel Lives
Blechhammer on the Oder
I'll See You Again
A Doctor and His Wife
Jack Shelley and the News
Alone Among Friends
Eden So Near
Meanwhile at Home
Life With Alexander
First the Black Horse
The Rise and Fall of Franklin D. Roosevelt
Against the Grain: Six Men Who Helped Shape America
Criminals and Folk Heroes: Gangsters and the FBI
The Clue is Grammar
Pickle Barrel and Mushroom: Atom Bombing
Lovers and Other Liars
Shuttle Bombing in WWII
The Doctor Decides

Assaulting the Riviera, 1944

Assaulting the Riviera, 1944

ROBERT UNDERHILL

Deeds Publishing

Copyright © 2020—Robert Underhill

ALL RIGHTS RESERVED—No part of this book may be reproduced in any form or by any electronic or mechanical means, including information storage and retrieval systems, without permission in writing from the authors, except by a reviewer who may quote brief passages in a review.

Published by Deeds Publishing in Athens, GA
www.deedspublishing.com

Printed in The United States of America

Cover design by Mark Babcock.

ISBN 978-1-950794-18-8

Books are available in quantity for promotional or premium use. For information, email info@deedspublishing.com.

First Edition, 2020

10 9 8 7 6 5 4 3 2 1

*To my beloved granddaughter, Caitlin Mills,
with admiration for her determined spirit*

INTRODUCTION

The Roman orator Cicero once warned, "Never begin with an apology."

Nevertheless, it may be warranted to alert readers of this book. Readers will not find a neat pattern of chapters developed along chronological or topical lines. Attempting to present such an arrangement in recounting a modern military invasion would be as futile as trying to eat soup with a fork.

War is chaos with aims muddied, lives disrupted, and innumerable orders which may arise more from personal quirks of commanders than from objective analysis. Weather and terrain play their parts, and different scenes take place at the same time. Like love affairs, wars have foreplay, and its after effects are left to scribes and historians.

The invasion of Southern France in the summer of 1944 was no exception; it was complex and confusing, a kaleidoscope of happenings. In the following account, nations with their diplomats and navies, armies, generals and admirals, seamen and soldiers, along with cooperative citizens will be mentioned. Some events will be under emphasized and others may appear out of sequence.

The account of this significant episode of WWII has been penned two and a half decades after the events occurred. The narrative is not offered as a personal memoir, and its author chooses to write in the third person because he was an observer and very minor participant in some of the action.

A reader might not like finding his hero had a few warts, and villains were not all bad. Maneuvers well-planned or otherwise failed or succeeded, and thousands of personal experiences may go unrecognized. That was the way it was.

An author can only do his best as he seeks your interest along with your tolerance. This one now shuts down his computer and returns to his couch for dreamier reminiscences.

—Robert Underhill

"There was no development of that period which added more decisively to our advantage or aided us more in accomplishing the final and complete defeat of German forces than did this attack coming up the Rhone Valley {from the Riviera}."

—General Dwight D. Eisenhower

1

THE BUILDING STORM

The northern shores of the Mediterranean Sea make up a territory commonly called the Riviera, some of the world's most beautiful scenery. Understandingly, the territory has been targeted by different invaders throughout centuries, and so it was during WWII.

The First World War brought down many of the royal houses of Europe and altered the nature and the calendar of the Riviera. Following that war, greater numbers of Americans began arriving, with business moguls and celebrities outnumbering aristocrats. The high society moved from a winter season to a summer season. While Europe was still recovering from WW I and the American dollar was strong, American writers and artists started arriving on the Côte d`Azur. Edith Wharton wrote *The Age of Innocence* (1920) at a villa near Hyéres; Isadore Duncan frequented Nice and Cannes, and the writer F. Scott Fitzgerald first visited the area with his wife Zelda, eventually staying at Saint-Raphael, where he wrote most of *The Great Gatsby* and got started on *Tender is the Night*.

World War II started on September 1, 1939, when the German Wehrmacht sent armed troops east across the border into Poland. In fulfillment of an earlier pact, England and France were forced to join the ensuing conflict in support of Poland, and for two and a half years war was waged on continental Europe and in submarine attacks against shipping in the Atlantic. Most of the shipping originated in the United States, where isolationists and their opponents passed confusing laws which consistently drew the country ever closer to actual military involvement.

By 1944, along the French Riviera there were no wealthy Parisians lolling on the white beaches that in peacetime had been a favorite playground for American millionaires, Russian grand dukes, and English lords with their ladies. The town of Saint-Tropez with its tall pink houses overlooking the protected bay where in prewar days the British Mediterranean fleet used to anchor was strewn with barbed-wire barricades. Every settlement along the coast was filled with squads of German soldiers marching the cobbled streets. Because of the soldiers' uniforms, non-Germans nicknamed the marchers *Feldgrau*, field gray.

ASSAULTING THE RIVIERA, 1944

In this fifth year of WWII, air raid sirens all along the coastline wailed when America's big four-engine B24s and B17s, as well as twin-engine fighter bombers, pounded German installations, radar stations, gun batteries, troop barracks, or headquarters. Not only Saint-Tropez but adjoining towns like Nice, Cannes, and the port of Toulon were deluged with explosives.

The military outlook for the Allies was very dark. In two weeks the German mechanized army had smashed through Poland in a *blitzkrieg* without parallel. In early April, 1940, the so-called "phony war" came to a dramatic end, and without warning, Germany took over Denmark, following that coup by moving into Norway. A month after the invasion of Scandinavia came another blow to the West; German forces invaded Belgium and neutral Holland. In five days the Netherlands were conquered. By the third week of May 1940, Nazi troops had reached the English Channel, cutting off a British expeditionary force that had been rushed there hoping to aid Belgium and France.

In June, Mussolini declared war on France, and five days later the *Gestapo* backed by German soldiers captured Paris. A hastily formed French government sued for peace, and Hitler got his revenge for a defeat suffered twenty-three years earlier. The Nazi Wehrmacht in one month had done what the Kaiser's forces had been unable to accomplish in four years.

2

In America during President Franklin Roosevelt's first term, his main concern, along with that of millions of fellow citizens, was on economic recovery. Much of the nation was still "ill-housed, ill-fed, and ill-nourished." Congressional committees had investigated the role of ammunition makers in World War I and journalists ballyhooed the findings to a point where a majority of U.S. voters looked askance at the war clouds gathering over foreign lands.

President Roosevelt swam with the isolationist tide although in October 1937 after Japan's incursion into China, he spoke for a quarantine against aggressor nations. The *Wall Street Journal* blasted the idea with a headline warning: "Stop Foreign Meddling: America Wants Peace." The *Chicago Tribune* and the *Hearst Press* were equally caustic.

FDR's suggestion, however, was enthusiastically

endorsed everywhere overseas except in Tokyo and Berlin, and mail at the White House ran four to one in favor of the concept. Foreign policies were fuzzy, but presidential rhetoric kept moving ever closer to alliance with England and France. Adding to foreign problems, FDR's second term would expire in 1940, and national elections were coming up. A third term was unprecedented, but to insiders it was clear he intended to run. Isolationist convictions were formidable, yet his allegiance was with Western Europe. A consummate politician, he worked both sides of the street.

When Congress met early in January, 1941, FDR appealed for support of nations who were fighting in defense of what he called the Four Freedoms—freedom of speech, freedom of religion, freedom from want, and freedom from fear.

The same week he spoke this appeal, Congress acquiescing to White House pressures passed legislation to circumvent existing limitations and make war materials immediately available to the Allies. Dubbed the Lend Lease Act, the legislation set off more acrimony, reaching its nadir in the Senate, where Burton K. Wheeler of Montana charged the move would "plow under every fourth American boy."

Lend Lease became the "arsenal of democracy," supplying Western Allies with more than $50 billion in arms, foods, and services. Events moved rapidly; public opinion hardened, and most U.S. citizens acquiesced when President Roosevelt ordered the navy "to shoot on sight" any German submarine encountered.

In Europe, the war continued to worsen for the Allies. German armor had reached the Channel coast, slicing France in two, while *Deutsche Panzer* units had wheeled north to Dunkirk, pinning more than 350,000 men of the British and Belgian armies against the sea.[1]

The outlook for Britain and France was somber, moving toward disaster with the inevitability of a Greek tragedy. When the second week of June 1940 began, President Roosevelt was in a train steaming toward Virginia. He had with him a prepared commencement address to be delivered at Charlottesville, Virginia, where his son Franklin, Jr. was graduating from law school. While entrained, FDR got word that Italy, not wanting to miss out on spoils the Nazis were gaining, had joined the fray and had declared war on France. Roosevelt in a voice larded with sarcasm overrode objections from his State Department and *ad libbed* a sentence to the prepared manuscript: "On this tenth day of June, 1940, the hand which held the dagger has struck it into the back of its neighbor."

The metaphor was a sensation and placed the American President shoulder to shoulder with Britain and France. Prime Minister Winston Churchill immediately cabled his enthusiasm and predicted that America's commitment would raise hope for all those who were resisting Nazi tyranny.

Rhetoric though did not stop the Nazis. The *Deutsche Wehrmacht* overwhelmed French forces and in the middle of June 1940 entered and controlled Paris. Two weeks later a joyous Adolph Hitler sat in a railway car in the Forest of Compiégne, the very place where the armistice in 1918 had been signed. He was there to avenge a defeat suffered 22 years earlier and now wanted to savor the surrender of his French foe.

President Roosevelt had watched events in Europe and Asia, and in 1938 had proposed to the British a conference of leading powers to be held in Washington where the underlying causes of turmoil in Europe could be addressed. British Premier Neville Chamberlain brushed him off saying he preferred an appeasement policy toward the aggressors.

The next year FDR sent personal messages to Hitler and Mussolini, asking them for promises not to attack any of the small countries of Europe for at least the next ten years. Hitler answered with an insult before ridiculing the request and larding his own report to the *Reichstag* with enough sarcasm to set off wild demonstrations by his assembled henchmen.

Mussolini at first refused to read the message and

then sneered at it, telling underlings it must have been "a result of infantile paralysis."

Nazi triumphs kept mounting throughout the summer of 1940; war news got more distressing every week. In England, Chamberlain's government failed and was replaced by doughty Winston Churchill, who upon taking office announced he had nothing to offer his country but "blood, toil, sweat, and tears." There were plenty of those in May 1940 when 350,000 British fighters along with much of the French army and Belgians were pushed back to the sea off the coast of Dunkirk in northern Belgium.

Churchill in London praised the gallantry of his countrymen who in daring maneuvers had rescued so many of the forces trapped at Dunkirk. Then the new Prime Minister growled, "…but wars are not won by evacuations."

Happenings overseas provided campaign issues for the U.S. elections in November, 1940. The bleak outlook for the West had encouraged FDR to see himself more as Commander-in-Chief than the nation's Chief Executive. After conferences with Allied diplomats and advisors of his own, he ordered fifty destroyers, which he labelled "old age," to be transferred immediately to Britain. The ships were in harbors "by coincidence," he said, and could be turned over at once to the British navy.

Surprisingly, there was little public criticism; even his campaign foe Wendell Wilkie proclaimed "whole hearted support for the President in whatever action he might take to give opponents of force the material resources of our nation."[2]

3

Throughout 1940, President Roosevelt was forced to deal with domestic politics, and as a consequence, war in Europe, relations with Churchill, Lend Lease, and subsequent aid to Russia were acted upon quickly without exploring the consequences of such actions.

Deteriorating conditions in the Pacific were treated as lesser problems than those flooding Europe. Yet in the Pacific area Japanese militarists with encroachments resembling Hitler's Nazism were riding high. Western powers stood aside when Nipponese troops took over neighboring governments.

In 1939, Japanese forces captured Shanghai and quickly made life miserable for Americans and Europeans living there. President Roosevelt retaliated by imposing economic sanctions, hoping such action might make Japan's leaders stop, look, and listen. Later in that same year, he received almost unanimous approval from

American citizens when he denounced the existing treaty with Japan.

The next year more trouble in the Pacific came with the Tripartite Pact in which Japan formally joined the European Axis. The Pact stipulated that if any one of the three got into war the other two would pitch in. This Pact when collated with the fall of France guided Roosevelt into a "short of war" policy with three objectives: 1) help England fight the war, 2) gain time for American rearmament, and 3) restrain Japan by diplomacy and a show of naval strength.[1]

Japan invaded China in July, 1937. War between the two nations started in July of that year at the Marco Polo Bridge, ten miles west of Peiping. At first some observers regarded it merely a local contest between isolated military units, but soon it became clear that war ministers in the Empire of the Rising Sun had more grandiose plans. Three years later, in 1940, when the Tripartite Pact was signed, much of China still was putting up stubborn resistance. American policymakers stood aside watching diplomats with hopes that Nipponese citizens weary of the enterprise and its costs would force Japanese militants to abandon the invasion.

In Washington, President Roosevelt chose not to apply the Neutrality Acts to problems in the Pacific. To apply such legislation there, he argued, would bring us into dispute with Japan over our right to trade with the

Chinese. By not intervening, the U.S. could continue to send aid to Chiang Kai-shek's forces and Japan was free to buy arms or ammunition from America. Ignored was the fact that the Rising Sun Empire did not need either of those. What it wanted was oil, scrap iron, and other raw materials.

In August of 1941 when FDR and Churchill met in Argentia, Newfoundland, an opening item in their conference was what to do about Japan's aggressions. For more than a year, FDR had been trying to avoid a showdown in the Pacific, believing that confronting Japan would mean "a wrong war in the wrong ocean at the wrong time."

His opinion dominated but did not erase arguments within his Cabinet. Secretaries Stimson, Morgenthau, and Ickes were convinced that stronger measures, such as a total embargo on oil shipments, ought to be adopted.

Despite differing opinions from his Secretaries, FDR strove to avoid an embargo, fearing such an act would drive Japan farther into the Dutch East Indies and drag the U.S. into the Asian maelstrom. He could not hold out, however, and following Japan's invasion of Indochina he accepted a policy of limited sanctions, including an embargo of high-octane oil. Implemented by subordinates while FDR and Churchill were meeting in Newfoundland, the embargo quickly expanded into full-scale.

The expansion strengthened the arguments of Nipponese war lords. Japanese couriers said their country would not withdraw from China but would promise not to advance farther if the U. S. would rescind the policy. Japanese War Minister General Hideki Tojo gave his diplomats the last day of November, 1941, to arrange a settlement with the U.S. In the meantime, Japanese militants put in play their schemes for a secret air strike against Pearl Harbor.

For a time it seemed President Roosevelt was ready to accept Japan's promise of no further armed troop advances, but the stumbling block was China. Strong protests from Nationalist Chinese Leader Chiang Kai-shek kept hardening America's position.

During the first week in November 1941, the Japanese privy council meeting in the presence of the Emperor made the decision to go to war. At the time the privy council chose this strategy, in Washington, D.C. the Joint Board of the Army and Navy—precursor of the Joint Chiefs of Staff—met to review the Pacific situation.

The group agreed that the first objective of American foreign policy should be to defeat Germany. The conferees went further to advise President Roosevelt that "war between the United States and Japan should be avoided." Both George Marshall and Admiral Harold R. Stark, Chief of Naval Operations, emphasized that the U.S. simply was not prepared; they accompanied their admission with a warning that such action would greatly weaken ongoing efforts in the Atlantic to defeat Germany.

European matters seemed more urgent than relations in the Pacific, yet those worsened fast. Japan's case was presented to U.S. Secretary of State Cordell Hull and Secretary of the Navy Frank Knox by Japanese Admiral Kichisaburo Nomura who was joined in early November 1941 by Ambassador Saburo Kurusu.

Later that month, the two envoys put forth a proposal: if the U.S. would lift the embargo, Japan would agree to no further territorial expansion and withdraw its troops from southern Indochina. The proposal said nothing about Japan's incursions in China.

Clearly at odds with U.S. foreign policy, talks between Hull and the two Japanese ministers muddled more. The latter brought in a subordinate who was asked to type a garbled message from Tokyo. In Washington the subordinate was engaged in the artifice two and a half hours after Japanese forces had landed in British Malaya and an hour after bombs had fallen at Pearl Harbor. A date in infamy had come.

4

Wars provide heroes and villains, and WWII was no exception. From its battlefields and skies came heroes like Eisenhower, Omar Bradley, George Patton, Jimmy Doolittle, Sandy Patch, and Douglas MacArthur, to name a few. Yet it can be argued that George Catlett Marshall at staff headquarters in Washington was America's foremost soldier throughout the conflict.

Few persons have worn as many hats as George Marshall—Chief of Staff, Secretary of State, Secretary of Defense, and the main mover in smoothing-out inter-service rivalries in the historic unification of the armed forces soon after the close of WWII. His career was capped in 1953 when he was awarded the Nobel Peace Prize.

Son of a father who had built a prosperous coal business in Pennsylvania, Marshall as a lad decided to become a soldier when he enrolled at Virginia Military

Institute. Following graduation from there in 1901, he first served stints in the Philippines and the U.S.

America entered WW I, and Marshall sailed to France with the AEF, achieving recognition for his staff work in battles at Cantigny, St. Mihiel, and Meuse-Argonne. He was aid-de-camp to General Pershing from 1919 to 1924, and then served for three years in China. Returning to America, he first was commander of the Eighth Infantry and after that the Fiftieth Infantry Brigade. A brigadier general in July, 1938, he was appointed to a high level post in Washington and a year later was named Army Chief of Staff.

Soon after starting his second term, President Roosevelt began appointing different advisors, some of whom would have historic impact on events to come. One of the most significant was Marshall. During the four and a half years when the U.S. was officially at war, Marshall was the power behind the scenes, planning and choosing most military campaigns. Moreover, he remained after the war to become one of the nation's topmost diplomats.

As Chief of Staff he inherited a host of problems, many of which had roots that could be traced back before Nazi forces crossed Polish borders in September, 1939. A month prior to that fateful date, a Nazi-Soviet Pact had been signed, only to be broken two years later when Hitler flushed with successes in conquering

Denmark, Norway, the Low Countries, and in defeating France sent his troops into the Soviet Union marching toward Moscow through the Ukraine to the Caucasus, White Russia, and the Baltic Republics. Winter cold and counter thrusts by stubborn Russian defenders, as well as immeasurable Lend Lease aid, stopped the Nazis at Stalingrad, and Soviet troops began driving the Axis from all of Eastern Europe and the Balkans.

American citizens and the Administration in Washington followed events in Europe much more than the happenings in the Far East. Yet there, too, diplomacy had failed and was being replaced by widening conflict. The debacle came on December 7, 1941, when the Empire of the Rising Sun carried out its sneaky attack at Pearl Harbor. Four American battleships were sunk: the *Arizona, California, Oklahoma*, and *Utah*. The battleship *Virginia* settled in shallow water, and another, the *Nevada*, ran aground. Other battleships damaged were the *Pennsylvania, Maryland*, and the *Tennessee*. Four destroyers went to the bottom. In all, fourteen ships were either sunk or badly damaged, and 3,000 Americans lost their lives.

The next day, December 8, 1941, the U.S. Congress voted for war against Japan, and two days later Germany and Italy living up to the Tripartite Pact announced war on the United States. The U.S. Congress in response quickly passed a resolution declaring war against those three countries.

Throughout 1942 there was not much war news for Americans to cheer about, notwithstanding a daring air raid on Tokyo led by General Jimmy Doolittle. The foray had little effect on the war, but it gave a lift to spirits of citizens at home. Yet the nation's military pride suffered more shock as U.S. forces were shoved from island after island in the Pacific. Bataan collapsed following a hopeless stand by defenders at Corregidor. Some relief came in May, however, when a U. S. naval fleet defeated a Japanese armada in the battle of the Coral Sea, and again in June when torpedo bombers routed an enemy task force in the Battle of Midway.

As months sped by, Allied war strategy became more offensive, marked by landings in the Solomons and New Guinea. In the Mediterranean area, the Allies were beginning to take the offensive, marked by George S. Patton, one of America's most remarkable generals.

5

George Patton was a swaggering leader who often behaved in ways that would have gotten other officers dismissed; he was kept on despite his flaws, for he possessed exceptional strengths and offensive skills.

At the opening of 1942, Nazi troops led by Field Marshal Erwin Rommel, the Desert Fox, confronted the British Eighth Army in North Africa, commanded by General Bernard Montgomery. Rommel struck hard, pressing his foes to the neighborhood of Trobuk and capturing that city before going farther to do the same with Bardia and Matruh in Egypt.

Not until June of that year was the Axis march checked, the halt being achieved at El Alamein, 70 miles west of Alexandria. The British victory there forced Rommel to make a full retreat, and within two weeks Eighth Army soldiers had recaptured Bardia, Matruh, and Bengazi.

From then on, events moved rapidly. French troops that had fled their homeland when Germans moved into France and occupied its capital city were amassed in North Africa. In the same month, disaster for the Allies came at Kasserine Pass, the first encounter for Americans against Nazi forces. U. S. troops were halted and then thrown back by Rommel's *Afrika Korps.* U. S. reinforcements arrived soon, however, and Americans retook former positions, thus checking the German drive. The next month, U. S. Major General George Patton came to Cairo for his new assignment: command of the U. S. Seventh Army.

The new commander arrived in Cairo, knowing he had been recommended for a promotion that was not yet through official channels. Nevertheless, he pinned another star on his lapel and proceeded to whip his troops into the disciplines he wanted. A subordinate officer who would gain his own fame a decade later was Lt. Colonel Westmoreland, who wrote:

> Patton would parade around with his boots, yellow britches, his Ike Jacket, two pearl-handled revolvers, and a shiny helmet with three stars all over it. His jeep looked like a motorized Christmas tree sprinkled with stars.[1]

Patton was the consummate soldier. Born November

11, 1885, in San Gabriel, California, as a young boy he set his sights on a military career. Throughout childhood he heard or read countless stories of his ancestors' victories in the Revolutionary and Civil War. Determined to follow their footsteps, he enrolled at the Virginia Military Institute in 1904 and a year later transferred to the Military Academy at West Point, graduating from there on June 11, 1909.

During WWII in 1943 Patton rose to one of the highest points in his career when he employed daring assault tactics to lead the U. S. Seventh Army to victory in the Mediterranean campaign.

It was during this period that the persona of *Old Blood and Guts* became common coin. "Overlord," the invasion of Normandy, had been postponed for another year, but citizens in the U. S. and the British Isles were howling for action. Something had to be done, and the best place to start was from newly won Allied bases in North Africa. The plan selected was to overrun Sicily, cross the Strait of Messina, and work up the Italian peninsula.

On July 10, 1943, more than 250,000 American and British troops were put ashore on beaches southwest of Sicily. Americans wading ashore were from the Seventh Army led by Patton, and accompanying British forces were under command of General Bernard Montgomery. Italian and German defenders were caught off guard and quickly routed.

The smoothness with which these landings were carried off impressed the German high command, and the Seventh Army with Patton in its lead swept across Sicily with speed that matched Sherman's march from Atlanta to the sea in the U. S. Civil War. Patton's Seventh Army and British forces soon controlled 150 miles of coastline and substantial beachheads.

Patton, ignoring orders, moved his troops first into Palermo on the northwest shore of Sicily. There he set up headquarters in the ancient palace of Norman kings and then marched farther east to cross the Strait of Messina, gaining the toe of Italy.

In mid-1943 some of Patton's aura faded. In Sicily on August 3rd, he strode into the tent of an evacuation hospital and asked Pvt. Charles Kuhl sitting at attention on the side of his cot what was wrong with him. "I guess I just can't take it," responded Kuhl.

Infuriated, Patton flared up, swore like the trooper he was, and called Kuhl all kinds of coward. Then slapping the soldier across his face, he grabbed him by the neck and forced him out of the tent. Observers either intimidated by Patton's rank or too stunned to interfere hustled the private away.

Kuhl ultimately was diagnosed as suffering from chronic dysentery and malaria. One week later a similar incident took place. This time the victim was Paul Bennett huddled and shivering by his hospital bed. When

Patton asked him what he was suffering from, Bennett replied, "I guess it's my nerves, Sir."

"Your nerves, hell! You're just a Goddamned coward," Patton shouted. He slapped Bennett's face, knocking off the soldier's helmet and yelled, "Shut up your Goddamned crying. I won't have these brave men who have been shot at seeing a yellow bastard sitting here crying... You're going to fight. If you don't, I'll stand you up against a wall and have a firing squad shoot you on purpose."

Anger overcoming judgment, Patton reached for one of the pistols on his belt saying, "I ought to shoot you myself, you Goddamned whimpering coward."

This time subordinates broke up the imbroglio by stepping between the General and the unfortunate soldier. Investigations later revealed that Private Bennett was no coward and was in the hospital against his wishes; he had asked two days earlier to be returned to his artillery unit.

There was little question about facts of the incidents, but news about them did not leak out until November. The reports did not change opinions of German generals who continued to regard Patton one of the best among all Allied generals. However, in the U. S. from coast to coast citizen tempers went up like rockets when they learned an American general was behaving like a barroom bully.

News reporters had begun to refer to WWII as the war to end all wars, but Patton knew better. He knew too much history to believe in that fantasy. Even in throes of the worst battles he continued to read about military heroes. Accounts of Julius Caesar's battles in Gaul and Germany rose off the pages for him and he saw himself as part of the action. Indeed, to understand Patton's career one must recognize his strange psychological make-up.

A realist when it came to assessing numbers, positions, and strengths of his immediate foes, he saw himself as one of the great generals of history: crossing the Alps on an elephant with Hannibal, standing shoulder to shoulder with Alexander the Great, Julius Caesar, or Napoleon. Mixed with such fantasies was his strong religious Protestant faith and his belief in reincarnation.

Patton was convinced he had an unbreakable connection with supernatural forces. Helping that conviction had been a battle in which he said he had been too terrified to stand and fight. Then he looked up and saw faces of his dead grandfather and several uncles demanding that he stop being a coward.

On another occasion while a covey of French news reporters were accompanying him he gave them a tour of Roman ruins including its famed Coliseum, parade grounds, and drove to the exact spot where Julius Caesar had once pitched his tent.

When the slapping incidents in Sicily became public knowledge, General Eisenhower, now Supreme Commander of Allied Forces, was forced to discipline his unrestrained comrade. He ordered Patton to deliver a personal apology to Allied troops in Africa. Patton in full dress and adorned with all his medals obeyed, but after having done that he was relieved from command of the Seventh Army and ordered to London for a different assignment.

6

A truism tells us that often a person far from battle areas is able to put happenings there in better perspective than can soldiers on the ground, sailors on the sea, or airmen in the sky. Each of the latter is thanking God for sparing him and is glad to be still alive; he has no time to remember that scenes around him are only tiny bits of a larger war.

So it was with Captain Bob Underhill, bombardier of the Second Air Group in the Fifth Wing of the 15th U. S. Air Force stationed eight miles east of Foggia, Italy. The cocky twenty-four-year-old captain had been a sharecropper before he was eighteen, a traveling salesman in Dixie territories before being transferred to cover the states of New Mexico and Arizona. Then volunteering to become an Army Air Corps cadet, he had earned his wings and instructed other cadets for two years before going overseas. Because of his stateside experience, he quickly was made lead bombardier for the Second Bombardment Group of B17s in Italy.

While an instructor at Deming, New Mexico, Underhill had a special student, John D. Ryan. Ryan then was a lieutenant colonel—ranking as high as Deming's Executive Officer. Destined for a distinguished career, Ryan, a West Point graduate, already was a command pilot by the time he came to Deming.

Two and a half years later, in July, 1944, Ryan was a full colonel in command of the Fifth Wing consisting of B17s in Italy, and he came up from Bari to Amendola to fly as co-pilot on a mission in the area around Nice, France.

He greeted Underhill, asking him if he ever hit anything beside the ground and after that sally gathered his maps and was all business.

Briefing officers had told crews their primary target would be Savona, Italy, but if that were not chosen alternates could be any other nearby settlement on the Italian or French Riviera. The weather was good and gun emplacements at Savona were well camouflaged. No enemy fighter planes appeared, and there was only sporadic flak at the target, enough though to cripple one bomber and injure two gunners in another.

Every crew member aboard the attack force noted the mass of vessels gathered around Corsica and neighboring islands, yet because of the loss of only one plane, the mission was considered a success, almost Hollywood style. It was not until two weeks later that Underhill learned why the high-ranked Ryan had flown as a co-pilot. Primary purpose of that mission had not been to bomb whatever ships were in the harbor but to reconnoiter the coastline looking for army camps, gun emplacements, or whatever defenses the occupying Wehrmacht might have mounted.

An hour before midnight on August 14, 1944, Underhill and other crew members of the Second Bomb Group were given a light meal before going to the briefing room. Scuttlebutt had told them something big was afoot; that was no mere rumor. The invasion of Southern France was ready to launch.

"Make no mistake about it," a briefing officer warned. "This is a big operation. It's going to be an army and navy enterprise; strategic bombers are important, but only as supporting players."

The primary targets for the Second Air Group were a German airfield and barracks in the Tropetz Gulf twenty miles east of Toulon. Take off would be at 0230—three and a half hours before the usual time. The Group's twenty-eight planes would assemble at 6500 ft. and maintain formation and hold air speed at an indicated 150 mph.

A key point would be over Corsica where the Group was to kill time until daylight broke. Weathermen had predicted a scattered undercast at about 3,000 ft. in the target area. Pilots and bombardiers were told only visual bombing would be permitted and the actual bombing altitude was to be 13,000 ft.

Underhill learned he was not going to have his usual assignment as a mission's lead bombardier; this time that duty would be performed by Enoch Broyles. Broyles had been another one of Underhill's students two years earlier back in the States; now he was the bombardier Colonel Ryan had chosen for every combat mission he himself flew.

The reason for Ryan's earlier flight with the Second Bomb Group also was clear; he was going to lead the entire assault, and Underhill's ship with Captain Mark Chadwick pilot would be his deputy lead just under his right wing. All Underhill had to do was watch the bombs come out of Ryan's ship then immediately toggle out his own load.

In the bomb bay of each B17 was hung a cluster of thirty-eight 100 lbs. fragmentation bombs. Each bomb was made of highly compressed steel rings that upon detonation would shatter into hundreds of flying shrapnel meant to maim or kill victims caught on the ground.

The Second Group flew around Corsica and other islands as ordered before heading for the Riviera coast. Daylight was just breaking and in waters below the planes were scores of seagoing vessels, ships of every size and shape. Yet this armada giant as it appeared to airborne observers was a shadow of those at Normandy a month earlier.

Even though the invasion would be primarily a naval and infantry operation, the entire 15th Air Force was there in support. It seemed each Group of bombers had different signaling systems because one would be using flares and another wing lights. There was no flak and no enemy fighters. Underneath the four-engine bombers were medium ones from the 12th A.F. and other planes of every description — P38s, P47s, P51s and many navy fighters launched from the decks of carriers now behind the flight of airplanes. The fleet had sailed from ports at Oran, Naples, Taranto, and Brindisi, and it had taken them five days to assemble.

Shortly after the initial point where the Second Bomb Group turned to begin its bomb run, light flak arose but not enough to break up the formation. Every plane had its bomb doors open, and every toggalier had his finger on the switch watching for bombs to fall from the lead ship. The most common load for a B17 was twelve 500 lbs. armor piercing demolition bombs, but for this raid most of the ships carried fragmentation ones — bombs hung vertically and were ones less accurate in their trajectories than demolition bombs.

The bombs had hardly hit the ground before Colonel Ryan radioed the Group. "We've done our job; let's get the hell out of here. It's time for the navy and army to take over."

John Dale Ryan was born in Cherokee, Iowa, December 10, 1915. At the U.S. Military Academy he played varsity football and graduated from the Point in 1938. He attended pilot training at Randolph Field and received his pilot wings from there in 1939. Ryan remained at Kelly Field as a flight instructor for two years before going to Midland Air Field in Texas where he helped establish a bombardier training school.

In February 1944, he was sent overseas to the 15th Air Force in Italy where he first commanded the Second Bombardment Group. From that assignment as a full colonel he moved to Bari, Italy and took over command of the Fifth Bombardment Wing.

In October, 1944, two months after the initial Riviera assault, Ryan led a bombing mission in the Bolzano Pass, the rail route Germans relied on to move supplies and equipment from Munich to Vienna. Intelligence had predicted a milk run, but it had turned out otherwise. Flak was intense and Ryan was hit by it in his left hand, resulting in later amputation of three fingers. The loss earned him the nickname "Three Finger Jack."

Ryan returned to Texas in 1945 and participated in the Bikini Atomic Weapons tests. His rank and responsibilities continued to move upwards: Director of Materiel for the Strategic Air Command, Commander of

SAC's Sixteenth Air Force in Spain, Inspector General of the U.S. Air Force, Vice Commander in Chief of the Pacific Air Force, and finally U. S. Chief of Staff in August 1969.

General Ryan died of a heart attack at age 67 on October 27, 1983, while hospitalized at Lackland AFB and was buried with full military honors at the U. S. Air Force Academy Cemetery in Colorado Springs, Colorado.

7

In November of 1943, President Roosevelt, Churchill, and Generalissimo Chiang Kai-shek met in Cairo for a conference from which came a declaration that upon victory the Allies would be satisfied with nothing less than unconditional surrender.

From Cairo, Roosevelt flew to Teheran where he and Churchill conferred with Russian Premier Josef Stalin. The three leaders agreed on strategy for the war and named General Dwight D. Eisenhower Supreme Commander of the European invasion forces.

The next six months saw a gigantic buildup of navies, armies, and planes in the British Isles. Air supremacy had to be won and was attained by June, 1944. On the sixth day of that month—D-Day—the Allies invaded Europe and established beachheads at Normandy, France. Actual military phases of the invasion were planned by George Marshall and other American and

British generals before gaining approval from President Roosevelt and Winston Churchill.

As Supreme Commander of Allied Forces in Europe, General Eisenhower was slated to lead the largest invasion in world history, a feat that involved more than 4,000 ships, some 3,000 planes, and Allied troops which eventually numbered over four million.

Thought to be impenetrable, German defenses began to crumble under relentless assaults by the Allies, who captured St. Lo, France in the middle of July, 1944. Americans pushed farther into the Brittany peninsula, driving eastward toward Paris. In Washington, General Marshall was anxious to begin another integral segment of WWII strategy.

It was early in the summer of 1942 when Marshall first presented President Roosevelt with plans for the invasion of France, including a companion maneuver for the southern coast of that country. In early planning, the code name for the Normandy operation was *Sledgehammer*, and the southern coast invasion was called *Anvil*. It wasn't long before Allied planners believed opponents had learned the two words, so the codes were renamed. *Sledgehammer* became *Operation Overlord* and *Anvil* became *Dragoon*. Both were welcomed by Josef Stalin at the Teheran Conference in late July 1943.

Operation Dragoon though was controversial from the start; even the origin of its code name is debated. One version impossible to document is that Churchill was first to apply it to Southern France. *Dragoon* was an accepted word in the English lexicon — used as a noun for a soldier either afoot or on horseback but always armed with a musket. The noun preceded a verb which in vernacular meant to force a recalcitrant person or stubborn animal into action. According to the apocryphal version, Churchill, ever aware of the vital war materiel being given by the U.S., remarked that he had been *dragooned* into acceptance of this military operation.

Marshall and compatriots in Washington kept insisting on it; British counterparts disagreed, arguing against it on the grounds that it would divert military resources from Allied troops in Italy.

Churchill favored invasion of the oil producing regions of the Balkans, reasoning that an assault there would deny Germany the petroleum it needed, would forestall advance of the Red Army, and would give the Allies a superior negotiating position in post war Europe.[1]

Marshall had proposed invasion of southern France in the belief that such an operation should be carried out as part of the larger maneuver being planned for Normandy. At Teheran during their conference in late July of 1943, FDR told Soviet Premier Josef Stalin about Marshall's idea. Stalin endorsed it, advocating the operation as an adjunct of *Overlord*. To American leaders, it was clear that Stalin preferred to have the Allies farther west than the Balkans, which he considered to be in his zone of influence.[2]

Although President Roosevelt accepted Marshall's plan, the idea of invading southern France was not favored by all American generals and his British Allies. General Clark in Italy clamoring for more men and supplies was against it, and to his death would insist the Riviera assault was a mistake.[3]

Churchill also opposed it, arguing that such a landing ought to be farther east, somewhere near the head of the Adriatic. The doughty Britisher went further to assert that Allied armies in Italy could drive into the Balkans and then on into Hungary, Czechoslovakia, Austria, and from those conquests on into the Third Reich. If this were done, he argued, communism would not be able to encroach more in central Europe, and Western Powers would be in a favorable bargaining position vis-à-vis Soviet Russia for control of lands farther east than what might be gained from an attack on the Riviera.

Churchill's rhetoric could not overcome the men and wealth America was supplying, so the plan for invasion of southern France was moved from document to actual preparation. It would be largely a naval and infantry maneuver and would be led by Admiral H. Kent Hewitt and General Alexander Patch.

On paper, the Dragoon operation called for a three-division assault under control of Major General Lucian Truscott's VI Corps, a unit subordinate to Lt. General Patch's Seventh Army.

Truscott's troops were to seize a forty-five-mile stretch of the conquests on into the Third Reich. If this were done, he argued, communism would not be able to encroach more on central Europe and Western Powers would be in a favorable bargaining position with Soviet Russia for control of lands farther east than what might be gained from an attack on the Riviera.

Subordinate to Patch's Seventh Army were French forces commanded by *General of the Army Jean-Marie de Lattre de Tassigny* whose troops were to capture the ports of Marseille and Toulon, vital enemy supply bases for armaments, ammunition, clothing, and whatever else was necessary for the occupying Nazis.

Allied Headquarters and American leaders turned down proposals from General Charles de Gaulle, President of the French Committee of National Liberation, that a French general be the overall ground commander for the invasion. De Gaulle badly wanted to recover French military prestige, but he had few cards to play. A sort of compromise was reached when Tassigny was permitted to lead the French Army B which remained under Seventh Army control.

By late July of 1944, German military leaders had

come to believe that a landing somewhere in the Mediterranean was imminent, most likely along the French coast. The leaders had delegated responsibility for the ground defense of southern France to General Johannes Blaskowitz, commanding *Army Group B*. Blaskowitz along with General Friedrich Wiese heading the *Nineteenth Army* were the principal German military commanders.

The main ground force of the Allies would be the U.S. Seventh Army. In March of 1944, headquarters for the 7th Army had been in North Africa, and the choice then of Lieutenant General Patch to command it had been a fortunate one.

Alexander Patch was born in 1889 at Fort Huachuca, Arizona, the son of a cavalryman who was a West Point graduate and a veteran of several Indian wars. As an adolescent the boy was pugnacious and high-spirited, never backing down from a fight or tolerating any kind of bullying. With urgings from his father, the young lad applied for admission to West Point, graduating from there in June, 1913. With his new commission, he was assigned to the 18th Infantry Regiment in Texas and served with it until the beginning of WW I. In that conflict Patch gained command of the 18th Infantry Battalion and led his unit in the final offensive of a war that was hyped to end all wars. By the time the fighting ended, Patch had developed pernicious pneumonia.

With treatment he recovered enough to return to active duty, but he continued to suffer sporadic bouts of the disease which eventually would kill him.

Between the wars, Patch spent eleven years as a Professor of Military Science at different schools in Virginia. When the U.S. entered WWII, he was commander of the 47th Infantry Regiment at Fort Bragg, North Carolina. His first battle command came in early March, 1942, when he was sent to New Caledonia with orders from Admiral William Halsey to "eliminate all Japanese forces on Guadalcanal."[4]

In December, 1942, Patch was chosen to command the newly created XIV Corps, headquarters for control of all Army and Marine Divisions in Guadalcanal. Public awareness of his vital role in the hard won victory at Guadalcanal went almost unnoticed in the hoopla reporters gave to more publicity seeking officers. The omission didn't matter much to the self-effacing, thoroughly professional General Patch, and it would not be the last time such slights would occur. Yet his talents and contributions did not fail to impress the leaders above him.

After Guadalcanal, General Marshall recalled Patch to command IV Corps at Fort Lewis, Washington, and during his stint in that assignment, Patch collected a very cohesive, well-coordinated and loyal staff which served him well in campaigns ahead.

In March 1944, he was given command of the Seventh Army; at the time it was only a headquarters in North Africa. In his position, he would have tactical control of all Allied troops in the forthcoming Anvil (later dubbed Dragoon) invasion. Thus under his control would be soldiers from three continents for an invasion if not as large as Normandy, would be at least as bloody and deadly.

Within 24 hours, 50,000–60,000 troops along with more than 6,500 vehicles were to be disembarked, and Allied ground forces were to be aided by an aerial fleet of 3,470 planes, tactical ones based in Corsica or Sardinia and big four-engine bombers from the 15th AF in Italy. Both tactical planes as well as the four-engine strategic bombers would pound bridges, air fields, traffic hubs, railroads, coastal defenses, and communication lines a week before the actual invasion took place.

The primary landing force would be General Patch's U.S. Seventh Army, and after the initial landing was assured, the French army led by General Jean de Lattre de Tassigney would take over with help from French Resistance units known as the French Forces of the Interior (FFR). These French Resistance units played a major role in the invasion of southern France—a role often ignored by western journalists.

Opposition troops were expected to be tied down by the invading units, which also would destroy bridges and communication lines, seize important traffic hubs, and directly attack isolated German forces. An integral role given to the Free French Forces was to carry out commando raids destroying guns of German garrisons on small islands just off the coast.

Two FFR units were given special assignments put into use to when main forces began approaching the beachhead. One was to render support by forming a diversionary flank, and the other would drop dummy parachutists and fake artillery pieces to disperse Wehrmacht defenders from the actual landing zones.

The main ground force would be the U.S. 7th Army, and the first American troops to land would be those of VI Corps led by Major General Lucian Truscott. These would be followed by the French Army B headed by General Jean de Lattre de Tassigny.[5]

The Naval Task Force for *Anvil* was under the command of Vice Admiral Henry Kent Hewitt, whose mission was to land the 6th U. S. Army Group. Formed in Corsica and activated a mere two weeks earlier, the 6th Army was expected to consolidate American and French forces.

Admiral Hewitt's naval support for the operation included: 1) three American battleships—*Nevada*, *Texas*, and *Arkansas*, 2) the British battleship *Ramillies*, and 3) the French battleship *Lorraine*. Along with these big ones were twenty cruisers for gunfire support and aircraft from nine carriers.[6]

The main ground force would be the U.S. 7th Army, and the first American troops to land would be those of VI Corps. The craft belched out from the VI Corps were ugly but formidable. The clumsy-looking contraptions with high steel gunnels mounted over six wheels made the craft look more like road-building tractors than sea-going vessels. Aboard each of them were infantrymen holding bayonetted M1 rifles, Thomson machine guns, heavy Browning Automatic Rifles, bazookas, or flame throwers—every kind of weapon known in modern warfare.

Men huddling below the gunnels unstrapped steel helmets, chewed gum, and mouthed silent prayers. Within a half-mile of the beach, the vessels stopped and opened their bows to vomit the armed fighters.

The VI Corps under control of General Truscott was to seize a forty-five-mile stretch of the coast east of Toulon. His assignment was supported by French forces which were to provide more than half the divisions for the operation.

The French II Corps, commanded by General Jean-Marie de Lattre de Tassigny, was clearly subordinate to the American Seventh Army headed by General Patch. Free French forces that had managed to escape

German invaders in their homeland and gather in North Africa were led by rival generals Henri Giraud or Charles de Gaulle. Both wanted to restore their nation's prestige and had urged that a French general be selected to lead the invasion, but they had few cards to play. Important as they were in the overall operation, French troops were not independent and could not go into action until ordered to do so by American generals Lucian Truscott, Jacob "Jake" Devers, or Alexander Patch.

8

Marshall and other leaders in the highest military echelon reasoned that the French did not understand American staff organization, procedures, supply, and evacuation systems, and with this conviction Marshall put Devers in charge, giving him the duty of aligning French and American forces. Devers had a free hand. He selected his own staff officers and liaison personnel and chose Henry Cabot Lodge, Jr., a Francophile with good political judgment, as his link with the French.[1]

French military man power was made up mostly by colonial levees drawn from north and central Africa—personnel who lacked technical skills and often were functionally illiterate. Thus whatever role they would play depended upon orders from General Devers and General Patch, the superior officers.

Both these leaders expected considerable help from French civilians—partisans who had proved their value as intelligence sources long before *Anvil* got underway. Such guerrillas were especially effective in disrupting communications and harassing defensive rear areas of the Nazi Wehrmacht. Although the Free French Forces had a voice in the Anvil invasion, it was only as loud as American and British generals allowed it to be.

The British had nourished carefully the FFR since the fall of France, but by mid-1944 American support equaled or surpassed British efforts. The FFR could put 75,000 men in the field, but only about a third of them were armed. These activists, known as the maquis, were backed by thousands of part-time supporters in cities, towns, and villages.

Maquis is a word that originated in Corsica, where it referred to thick underbrush. That island's brigands living in isolated elevations were known as *maquisards*. Under Hitler's fascist occupation the term soon was applied to dissident elements geographically separated from French society.

Rural conditions in southern France were ideal for the maquis; mountains and forests provided fresh water, game, and sunshine plus the fact that here the Nazis were not as numerous as in Normandy up north.

The maquis were not formidable enough to engage enemy troops in open warfare, but they severely limited freedom of movement by their Nazi foes by pestering their support organizations and interfering with placements of their tactical units. Moreover, sabotage by the maquis forced the Germans to employ large numbers of troops to repair rail, highway, telephone, and telegraph communications. [2]

Staff Sergeant Audie Murphy declared, "I've heard a lot of people say the landings in southern France were soft. That's not true. We had plenty of trouble, and the fighting was tough.[3]

When the Nazi invasion of France started expanding toward regions in the southern parts of that country, Wehrmacht forces were met near Grenoble by French troops aided by men and women from the civilian population. In June of 1940, Grenoble was being accepted as a part of the French State, a condition which lasted for two years until Mussolini's invaders came in to take over.

The area was extremely active in Résistance movements. One of the city's major universities supported clandestine operations and helped prepare false documentation for young men and women to prevent them from being picked up and assigned duties by whatever occupying force was then in control.

Sisteron, a community on the banks of the Durance River, had been inhabited for more than a thousand years. Roman soldiers used a route through it, and it escaped barbarian invasions after the fall of Rome. During the French Revolution the town remained

Royalist. Consequently, when Napoleon arrived on his march north after his escape from Elba in 1815, the town ignored him and let him pass through it.

In August, 1944, twin-engine French bombers and American four-engine Flying Fortresses attempted to destroy the railway bridge and its nearby road bridge, but the weather was bad and this first attempt failed. During this mission one bomber accidentally dropped several bombs on the town, including a church, causing more than a hundred casualties. Three days later on August 17th, French aircraft returned to wipe out the two bridges.

In September of the previous year, German management of Grenoble had harshened, and within one month angry citizens staged massive strikes and demonstrations in front of collaboration offices. In response, officials arrested more than 400 of the demonstrators. Such events only intensified Grenoble's opposition. Résistance operations mounted, and in the third week of August, 1944, when Allied troops were unmistakably heading for embattled Grenoble, German occupiers moved out enabling General Charles de Gaulle to enter and "recognize a heroic city at the peak of French resistance and its combat for liberation."

9

General Patch selected the 3rd, 36th, and 45th Infantry Divisions—all veterans of mountain fighting in Italy—to make the main ground attack, and his experience in training subordinate officers paid off handsomely when he selected the reliable Lucian Truscott to head it.

Alexander "Sandy" Patch was new to the Mediterranean theater, but he had compiled an impressive record that stretched back to America's frontier wars. At West Point he had been a classmate of George S. Patton, and after graduating from the Point had served with General Pershing's expedition into Mexico. Next came WW I in which he commanded a division with the AEF. In the interval between the two wars, he alternated between training schools and other peacetime assignments.

Early in 1942, George Marshall selected Patch to command troops headed for the South Pacific. Patch quickly whipped the gerry-built force into shape and with it assaulted the island of Guadalcanal. With one Marine division and two from the army, in two months he had rooted out the island's stubborn Japanese defenders.

Thin, wiry, and forthright, Patch spoke quickly, sometimes with sarcasm or dry humor. Yet he won respect from fellow officers as a steady, if quiet leader and a soldier's general, less concerned with prerogatives of command than he was with getting the job done. Throughout his career, he was always deeply moved by casualties suffered by those under his command; leadership demanded that personal tragedies be put aside.

No better example can be found than when on October, 1944 and he was immersed in invasion matters, his son, Captain Alexander M. Patch III, was killed in action. Despite profound shock and sorrow he buried his son at a military cemetery and a few days afterwards went back to winning the war. He wrote his grieving wife a bit of solace by saying their loss was far from unique; so many other parents suffered the same.[1]

Experiences gained through training officers paid off handsomely in 1944 when Patch, with approval from George Marshall, chose General Lucian Truscott as head of the main attack on the Riviera. Truscott would lead three army divisions bolstered by Free French Forces (FFR) and Canadian commandos. No newcomer to battle, Truscott had been a division commander in North Africa, and subsequently promoted to corps level command for his performance in the Anzio campaign. A cavalry officer earlier in his army career, Truscott was convinced that in military operations speed was absolutely essential.

For the Riviera assault, he picked three of the most experienced Divisions from the fighting in Italy. Each Division had attached to it a separate tank battalion, a self-propelled tank destroyer battalion, three battalions of corps artillery, and miscellaneous support units to keep all elements running after reaching the beaches.

Naval and amphibious phases of Anvil were commanded by Vice Admiral Henry K. Hewittt and along with his duty was integrating the U. S. Eighth Fleet with the British, French, Canadian, and Polish vessels making up what was labelled the Western Naval Task Force. On paper, he and General Patch had equal responsibilities, but until the latter was able to establish headquarters ashore, it was Hewitt who commanded both the ground and naval echelons.

10

Along the Riviera early in the morning of August 15, 1944, as dawn broke the eastern sky, mountains behind the coast were barely visible. Flights of B17s and B24s had winged overhead to drop their loads on the defenders. American Generals Patch and Truscott stood together on the bridge of their command ship, *Cactoctin* and watched the numerous vessels around them. The transports had been loaded in Naples or other Italian ports, and crews already had eaten hearty breakfasts consisting of steaks and fresh eggs — traditional mess for invaders. Then in darkness, soldiers had clambered into their assigned ships.

Not far distant, British Prime Minister Winston Churchill strode the decks of the fleet's flagship, the destroyer *Kimberly* having come to watch a landing he had opposed. He could detect no German fire coming off the beaches, and perhaps remembering daring ventures of his own, he regretted not having insisted on going ashore himself.[1]

Among assets at his disposal, General Patch could count on American and British parachute and glider troops to drop well inland of the beaches where they would be able to forestall reinforcement of defenders as well as prevent German retreats and could interrupt Nazi command and communication systems. Moreover, there were the French forces who were expected to provide more than half the divisions for the operation.

The British commander of the Mediterranean Fleet in March of 1944 informed General Henri Geraud of the intended operation, but after that very brief exchange, American and British leaders made the key decisions without consulting French officials, a practice that riled ever sensitive Francophiles. Giraud tried to assure his Allied companions that despite France's defeat four years earlier resulting in the fall of Paris, French troops subsequently had performed nobly in Italy and that there were plenty of competent French generals. Such arguments did not prevail.

De Gaulle lost his argument but won a slight compromise. General Jean-Marie de Lattre de Tassigny was given temporary command of the French II Corps which would remain under control of the U.S. Seventh Army and its leader, General Patch.[2]

Important as they were in the overall operation,

ASSAULTING THE RIVIERA, 1944

French troops were not independent and could not go into action until ordered to do so by American Generals Truscott, Jacob "Jake" Devers, or Alexander Patch.

Jacob "Jake" Devers, a field artillery man, had been born in York, Pennsylvania in 1887. A West Point graduate, he had taught at various posts and had missed any combat experience in WW I. In early 1940, General Marshall tapped him with his first star, and Brigadier General Devers joined the War Department. Promotions followed, and in May 1943, he was awarded his third star. Marshall sent him to London as commanding general of the European Theater of Operations (ETO), but when Eisenhower was named Supreme Commander of the Allied Expeditionary Force, Devers was moved to the Mediterranean area.

The smoothness with which the first Allied landings in the Mediterranean theater had been carried out impressed German high command, and the Seventh Army with George Patton in its lead swept across Sicily. Patton's Seventh Army and British forces soon controlled 150 miles of coastline and substantial beachheads.

General Mark Clark at the time ranked high in the estimate of Supreme Commander Dwight Eisenhower, who in January of 1943 put him in command of the Fifth Army based in North Africa. Clark did not participate directly in the Riviera assault; in fact up until his death he argued that the operation had been a mistake that robbed him of armaments, troops, food, and supplies with which he could have captured all of Italy.

Mark Clark, son of U.S. Army Colonel Charles C. Clark, was born on May 1, 1896, in Watertown, New York. Following his father's footsteps, Mark entered West Point in 1913 and graduated from there four years later. Commissioned in the army, he served in World War I and was wounded in France. When that war ended, Clark remained in the army and acquired additional training at the Infantry School's Advanced Officers Course at Fort Benning, then the General Staff College at Fort Leavenworth in 1933, and the Army War College in 1936.

Subsequently posted to Fort Lewis, Washington, he renewed acquaintance with George Marshall with whom he had served in France. When Marshall was named Chief of Staff, he chose Clark as Assistant Chief of Staff for Operations, and in August of 1941, three and a half months before Pearl Harbor, Clark was promoted to brigadier general, the youngest army general at that time.

Among the soldiers under his command was the 100th Infantry Battalion, made up with Japanese Americans from Hawaii. Initially rejected by Eisenhower, Clark took them on with enthusiasm. In his autobiography he recalled that the 100th Infantry Battalion was one of the Fifth Army's most valuable assets, adding, "The Nisei troops seemed very conscious of the fact that they had an opportunity to prove the loyalty of thousands of Americans of Japanese ancestry... I was proud to have them in the Fifth Army."[3]

Although General Eisenhower thought highly of him, others who worked with Clark did not always share that opinion. In his diary, George Patton wrote, "It makes my flesh creep to be with him.[4] Patton's opinion of Clark was borne out in the fall of 1943.

In September of the next year, American and British forces landed at Salerno, thirty miles southeast of Naples. It was Mark Clark's first battle command in the war. Compared with other landings in Europe and the Pacific, the German defense at Salerno was not particularly fierce, yet it was enough to drive Clark to near panic. When he told a compatriot he was considering pulling out, his British Superior, General Harold Alexander, overruled him, saying, "There will be no evacuation. We'll proceed from here." That order put an end to Clark's dalliance to retreat.

In September 1943, Clark, in command of the Allied Fifth Army, was given two British and two American infantry divisions and ordered to invade Italy at the earliest possible date. The assault force took off heading for Salerno from ports between Oran and Alexandria. A short wave message to the force from General "Ike" broadcast news of the Italian surrender. Men in the assault force were elated, believing the capture of Salerno would be a milk run.

Yet the best officers who served under Clark came away with their doubts, and several noted that in a crisis he would blame everybody but himself.

Mark Clark had spent most of his youth at Downers Grove, Illinois near where his father was stationed at Ft. Sheridan. In June 1913, the young lad received an appointment to West Point and graduated from there four years later along with his commission as a second lieutenant. He ranked 110th in a class totaling 139 and chose the infantry as his branch.

With expansion of the army in WW I, he rose quickly—first lieutenant in May 1917 and captain two and a half months afterwards. He went overseas and was with the AEF in the area of the Vosges Mountains when he was wounded. It took six weeks for him to recover, but at the end of that time he was declared unfit for return to the infantry. Instead he was assigned to the Supply Services of the First Army.

During the period between the wars, Clark served in a variety of staff or training roles. In August 1941, four months before fateful Pearl Harbor, he was passed over the rank of colonel and given his first star—a brigadier general. In April of the next year he was in England working with General Dwight Eisenhower on the feasibility of a cross channel invasion of German occupied Europe.

Eisenhower at the time was Commander of Allied Forces in the Mediterranean Theater, and he selected Clark as one of his deputies. Ike appreciated Clark's services, and that appreciation blossomed in November 1942 with the promotion of Clark to lieutenant general. Patton, both older in age and senior in rank, had come to regard Clark as "too damned slick" and overly impressed with himself. The impression had been gained in part when General George Marshall accompanied by Clark had come to Patton's headquarters to talk over plans for invasion of Sicily. Patton had decided to tolerate his younger colleague, but in his daily journal noted an unfavorable impression. Using his customary salty language, *Old Blood and Guts* added: "If you treat a skunk nicely he won't piss on you — as often."[5]

Americans captured Naples in October 1943, and were able to seize control of airfields on the other side of the peninsula. From Naples to Rome is a mere 100 miles, but Allied armies with numerical superiority in land forces and supremacy in the air could not take the territory. Ground fighting between Fifth Army soldiers and forces commanded by German General Marshal Albert Kesselring was fierce and indeterminate. American war correspondent Ernie Pyle described the conflict as "almost inconceivable misery." He went further to write that in mud and frost, G.I.'s "lived like men of prehistoric times, and a club would have become them more than a machine gun."[6]

Battle over Allied shipping and Nazi U-boats delayed the planned invasion of continental Europe. That historic event had to be postponed until the beginning of summer 1944, yet citizens in America and the British Isles clamored for aggressive action of some sort.

Well aware of the need to bolster citizen support, George Marshall in Washington had developed an ancillary operation to augment the *Overlord* invasion. The strategy was to mount another invasion that would put more Allied troops ashore on continental Europe as well as drain German defenders at Normandy.

11

The Italian Campaign of WWII consisted of Allied operations in and around the peninsula between 1943 and 1945. In the Mediterranean area no battles, including those in North Africa, cost more than Italy in terms of lives lost and wounds suffered by infantry forces on both sides during bitter fighting around strong points at Winter Line, the Anzio beachhead, and the Gothic Line.[1]

It is estimated that between September 1943 and April 1945 somewhere between 60,000 and 70,000 Allied and German soldiers died. The number of Allied casualties was about 320,000 and the German figure, excluding those who perished in the final surrender, was put at 330,000.[2]

Even before British victories in North Africa in 1943, there was disagreement among the Allies as to the best strategy for defeating the Axis. The British under Churchill's advocacy put forth their historic naval-based plans. The traditional British attitude when facing a continental enemy was to form a coalition and with it mount operations designed to weaken the foe.

U. S. strategists favored putting their larger armies into direct confrontation with the opposing forces. Most American staff officers believed a full-scale invasion of France at an early date was necessary to end the war in Europe; British counterparts rebutted that troops trained for landings in the Mediterranean Theatre was not only possible but would lessen pressures on the primary invasion across the Channel.

British and U. S. leaders eventually compromised; both would commit the bulk of their forces for the invasion at Normandy while launching a smaller campaign in the Italian Peninsula. If Italy could be overrun and knocked out of the war, Allied naval forces would then dominate the Mediterranean. The Allies then would have use of vital ports such as Toulon and Marseille on the French Mediterranean coast and greatly increase pressure against Nazi foes by opening another front.

12

Well aware of the need to bolster citizen support, George Marshall, Chief-of Staff in Washington, developed an ancillary operation to augment the *Overlord* invasion. The strategy was to mount another invasion that would put more Allied troops ashore on continental Europe, as well as drain German defenders at Normandy.

Allied plans were to use troops from North Africa to overrun Sicily, taking first Palermo and then crossing the Strait of Messina before attacking the toe of the Italian mainland. The strategy, if successful, would give the Allies control of the Mediterranean and knock Italy out of the war.

The assault began on July 10, 1943. Caught by surprise, German and Italian defenders of Sicily were overwhelmed. The American Seventh Army led by the swashbuckling General George Patton, together with British forces under command of General Bernard

Montgomery, soon controlled 150 miles of coastline and substantial beachheads. The Germans could only try delaying actions, and the Italians decided it was time to quit. Negotiations for Italy's capitulation dragged on until September when General Eisenhower could broadcast news of the surrender.

Not long after the Italian surrender, General Truscott organized a light mechanized combat unit of American men assigned to his VI Corps and named Frederic Butler, a brigadier general, as its leader. Designated Task Force Butler (TFF- Butler), the unit included one cavalry squadron, two tank companies, one battalion of motorized infantry, supporting artillery, tank destroyers, and other ancillary forces.

Born four years before the turn of the century, Butler had served previously as assistant commander of the 34th Infantry Division. His new command, usually referred to as the Butler Task Force, consisted of an infantry battalion, a cavalry reconnaissance squadron, two companies of medium tanks and one of tank destroyers, a field artillery battalion, and other assorted units.

On the evening of August 12, 1944, the entire assault corps was afloat—3rd, 36th, 45th Infantry Divisions and their supporting units. At 9:00 P.M. Truscott was piped aboard the command ship *Catoctin* for a conference called by General Patch who was awaiting him. Also aboard with Patch were Admiral Kent Hewitt and

General Gordon Saville, leader of the 12th Air Force whose planes would provide tactical support for the invaders.

When Truscott moved from gangplank to deck of the *Catoctin*, Patch greeted him. Twenty minutes later, the ever sensitive General Patch knowing that no officer leading an offensive liked to have a superior with him observing every move said to his subordinate, "Truscott, I am coming along on the *Catoctin*, but I want you to know I do not intend to embarrass you in any way. I am not going to interfere in the way you fight your battle. I want you to know it."

Truscott moved by the promise gave a tactful reply. "Thank you, General. I have no desire but to work with the closest possible cooperation, and I'll always be glad to have your advice."[1]

General Butler was fuming in the early morning of August 18th; his bold cavalry sweep less than an hour old had been stopped by German defenders who had put up steel rails and cables, posts, boulders, anti-tank mines, and two hundred pounds of explosives to block any passage. A day earlier, Truscott had given Butler oral orders to push northwest to the town of Sisteron on the Durance River—an advance of about fifty miles—and left it to Butler to choose his route.

Rather than heading immediately for Sisteron, Butler decided to swing west to a point on the Durance River lying south and west of Sisteron. From that spot, Butler's forces could approach Sisteron from the southwest rather than from the southeast, a trek over a mountainous terrain in which a handful of men could halt any advance.

Butler's forces were advancing over his chosen route when a spotter plane reported that a bridge on the route had been blown. The pilot advised Butler to send his columns through a winding bypass in the hills.

Along with Butler's Task Force was a French maquis liaison officer, and General Butler gave him the assignment of ejecting all Germans defending the bypass. Maquis and local sympathizers were quick to support the endeavor.

Slowly, the ranks of the Task Force were swelled by additional reinforcements—armored field artillery and a half dozen more tank destroyers. Even in the face of these reinforcements, the Germans were amassing defenses. Butler radioed Truscott for help, and the latter immediately dispatched the 141st Infantry Regiment for the critical job.

His troops succeeded in blocking the Rhone highway but still faced dangers from the rear. Butler and his men were able to drive back a battalion of German infantry from the *305th Grenadier Regiment*. His forces kept pushing forward, and when American GIs entered the town of Loriol a company of the *757th Grenadier Regiment* defending it surrendered. [2]

13

By August of 1944, Task Force Butler controlled the hills north of the town of Montélimar. Everything was not rosy, however, for the Germans had succeeded in isolating Task Force Butler from supplies. For several days, Allied men and supplies trickled in. The first units of the 36th Division arrived, and Task Force Butler was officially dissolved to be absorbed in the newly-arrived 36th Infantry Division commanded by Major General John E. Dahlquist.

With experienced fighters in his reorganized Division, Dalquist attempted a direct attack against Montélimar, only to have his move repulsed by the enemy's counter thrust. The aim of the German maneuver was to push Americans from the hills north of the town, thus forcing their artillery to move back out of range. The German action gained some ground temporarily but proved to be a failure when Allied troops stiffened and retook the ground Germans thought they had won.[1]

While on some beaches American GIs encountered little opposition, others were far different. St. Raphael beach saw some of the invasion's deadliest fighting. Three companies of experienced German *Grenadier Regiments* defended the beach that was pounded by more than a hundred B24 bombers. Landing craft were sent in but were halted a few yards offshore by orders from the navy.

Staff Sergeant Audie Murphy, who became the most decorated soldier of WWII, ran through whizzing bullets and found a machine gun crew. Borrowing their weapon he crawled forward far enough to kill two men, wound a third, and silence the formidable gun nest. Other Germans sprayed carbine fire at him, but he crept on, killing two more men and forcing the remaining five to surrender.[2]

Murphy was one of the men from Company B, 1st Battalion, 15th Infantry Regiment landing with the first wave near St. Tropez. Already decorated for bravery in the fierce fighting at Anzio in Italy, Murphy led his platoon inland until they were driven to ground by machine gun fire from a ridge confronting them. Then backtracking until reaching an American machine gun crew, he borrowed one of their weapons and raced back to his own platoon. He told his men to stay put and let him crawl ahead to take out the enemy's machine gun nest.

Murphy set up his machine gun and was just ready to fire when enemy soldiers waved a white flag. Alongside Murphy was his wartime buddy, Lattie Tipton, who stood up to accept the surrender but was cut down immediately by a blast of enemy fire. Murphy was so maddened by the perfidy that in intelligence briefings afterwards he confessed he couldn't remember much of what happened next.

His Distinguished Service Cross gives this account:

> Sgt. Murphy dashed alone toward the enemy's strongpoint, disregarding bullets that glanced off rocks around him and hand grenades that exploded as close as fifteen yards away. He closed in, wounded two Germans with carbine fire, killed two more in a fierce, brief fire fight, and forced the remaining two to surrender.[3]

Eight miles beyond the shoreline at St. Raphael, General Truscott at his command post contemplated how he could destroy the rest of the German forces there. Now was an opportunity to send a strike force toward Grenoble and from there to the high ground just upstream from Montélimar—his fondest hope when he had created the Butler Task Force.

Slowly, the ranks of the Task Force were swelled by additional reinforcements — armored field artillery and a half dozen more tank destroyers. Even in the face of these reinforcements, the Germans were amassing defenses. Butler radioed Truscott for help, and the latter immediately dispatched the 141st Infantry Regiment for the critical job. After these men had joined Butler's forces, he decided to mount the attack on Montélimar. His troops succeeded in blocking the Rhone highway but still faced dangers from the rear. That situation continued until 23rd of August when the Task Force was dissolved and its forces merged into the 36th Infantry Division of the Seventh Army. For a time General Butler was commander of the unit and three days later led it in driving back a battalion of German infantry from the *305th Grenadier Regiment*.

Veterans at Montélimar were not swilling champagne, however. Fighting for that key city had been too costly. A single battalion had lost twenty-four tanks with fifty-four men in their crews either killed or wounded. Final casualty lists showed that during one month more than 500 American comrades had been slain, wounded, or were missing in action.[4]

14

During the planning for Anvil/Dragoon, General Patch had given de Lattre's forces the mission of capturing Toulon, then Marseille. De Lattre seemed surprised at the assignment and responded, "General, you are giving me a tremendous task. Do you expect my army to accomplish both those missions?"

Patch replied, "Well, General, I feel that both Toulon and Marseille are French ports and cities of importance. The honor of their capture obviously should go to the French Army."[1]

A major reason for capturing Toulon and Marseille quickly was to prevent their almost certain destruction if German defenders were forced to retreat. Commando teams from French naval personnel had infiltrated both the cities in July to keep German enemies from destroying the docks or blocking the channels. A team in Marseille, for example, had succeeded in pouring concrete into primer ducts leading to preset charges, thereby preventing the ruin of several quays.

Within 24 hours, 50,000–60,000 troops along with more than 6,500 vehicles were to be disembarked. Allied ground forces were aided by a large aerial fleet of 3,470 planes, tactical ones based in Corsica or Sardinia and big four-engine bombers from the 15th AF in Italy. Both tactical planes as well as the strategic four-engine bombers had pounded bridges, air fields, traffic hubs, railroads, coastal defenses, and communication lines a week before the actual invasion took place.

The units were expected to tie down opposition troops by sabotaging bridges and communication lines, seizing important traffic hubs, and directly attacking isolated German forces. An integral role given to the FFR was to carry out commando raids destroying guns of German garrisons on small islands just off the coast.

Two FFR units were given special assignments to use when main forces began approaching the beachhead. One was to render support by forming a diversionary flank, and the other would drop dummy parachutists and fake artillery pieces to disperse Wehrmacht defenders from the actual landing zones.

As the sun began to peek over the eastern horizon on the morning of August 15, 1944, the B17s and B24s withdrew to let the battleships take over which they did by firing salvoes of bombs each weighing 500 lbs. or more. Then their firing stopped, and transports moved to within 1,000 yards of the shore before halting to open wide doors from which emerged clumsy-looking vehicles with two wheels over which heavy-linked chains powered by the tank's engines rolled constantly through the soft sands.

Inside each vehicle two dozen men wearing steel helmets crouched below the gunnels and mouthed their silent prayers. Each crouching infantryman was the most heavily laden man in the history of warfare. Added to the weight of his steel helmet might be an M-1 rifle, a knife, his canteen, a combination entrenching tool of pick and shovel, his bayonet, first aid pouch, a web belt with two cartridges in each pocket, two bandoliers of extra ammo, hand grenades hanging from handles on his suspender-belt, and the suspender harness supporting his pack which contained: a poncho, Primacord fuses, mess kit, cigarettes, a Zippo lighter, letters from home, and various rations—C, K, or canned ham and eggs.

The invaders would tie down opposition troops by sabotaging bridges and communication lines, seizing important traffic hubs, and directly attacking isolated German forces. An integral role given to the FFR was to carry out commando raids destroying guns of German garrisons on small islands just off the coast.

15

Most of the enemy forces defending target areas in Southern France were under command of German General Johannes Blaskowitz. His mission was to protect the two-thirds of France south of the east-to-west flowing Loire River.

General Johannes Blaskowitz and General Friedrich Wiese heading the *Nineteenth Army* were the principal German military commanders.

In mid-May of 1944, General Erwin Rommel had come down from his headquarters north of Paris and had rebuked Blaskowitz and other subordinate generals telling them, "We must have better defenses. Go all out to strengthen the *Südwall* (South Wall)—beginning immediately."

At the beginning of August, 1944, Blaskowitz sought

approval to rush the first-rate 11th Panzer Division from the Bordeaux region along the Atlantic seaboard to the Marseilles-Toulon area on the Riviera. There the formidable Panzer Division would be ready to launch an immediate counter attack if the Allies attempted to land on the beaches.

The Wehrmacht command structure was faulted, however, because *der Fuhrer* insisted that major decisions had to come only from his headquarters at *Wolfsschanze* (Wolf's Lair) in East Prussia. Thus the command system left battle commanders like Blaskowitz powerless to react until Hitler sent them whatever decisions were made at *Wolfsschanze*.

Moreover, *der Fuhrer's* strategy evolved in part from a very sophisticated subterfuge code-named *Operation Ironside* carried out by a British security team. The aim of this ploy was to convince Hitler that the Bordeaux region on the Atlantic coast –not the San Raphael region farther east—was likely to be invaded.

The *Ironside* ruse hoodwinked Hitler and his advisors so well that the 11th Panzer Division was still sitting idle at Bordeaux on August 12th when German reconnaissance pilots reported to General Blaskowitz that they had seen an armada of more than seventy-five to a hundred vessels, including what looked like troop transports, steaming along the coast of Corsica.

Other German intelligence agents reported that an

army group led by General Patton was being put together in southeastern England. At his headquarters in Prussia, Adolph Hitler could not be swayed from his belief that such a force was being readied for a cross channel invasion. In actuality, reports of the phantom force were created and spread by the nimble minds of British agents.[1]

Exact locations for the Anvil landings were determined by two factors: (1) the need to secure ports like Toulon and Marseille, and (2) determination to avoid a disaster such as Anzio in Italy where Wehrmacht control of the high ground had kept the Allies under continued enemy fire.

The Riviera coastline is not a smooth line of sandy beaches running from Marseille and Toulon on the west to Cannes more than a hundred miles east. Many prospective beaches lacked good exits, and most could be blocked by German defenders.

Aware of these liabilities, Allied planners from the Seventh Army and Western Task Force chose to attack the shoreline extending from Cape Cavalaire, thirty miles east of Toulon, northeastward another thirty miles to Anchor Cove, eight miles beyond St. Raphael. The Seventh Army would have to capture the high ground quickly before German reinforcements that could overwhelm the invaders.

The chosen site had other hazards. Its thirty miles

of coastline, for example, translated to more than fifty miles of irregular cliffs and outcroppings.

When August, 1944 began, life was not too harsh for most French citizens along the Riviera. The Nazi swastika had flown over most public buildings, and General Friedrich Weise, Commander of Germany's Nineteenth Army, lived very comfortably. Unlike Paris, the French capital up north where the population was on a starvation diet, here in this agricultural region was adequate food for troops and citizens.

Yet General Blaskowitz at his headquarters across the Ligurian Sea and near Toulon had become increasingly frustrated. He had sought approval from higher commanders to rush the experienced 11th Panzer Division now billeted on the Atlantic Seaboard to the Riviera where they could launch an immediate counter attack if the Allies tried to invade, but seven days had passed while he cooled his heels waiting for answers which never came.

Shortly after D-Day at Normandy, German Field Marshal Gerd von Rundstedt delegated responsibility for the ground defense of southern France to Generals Johannes Blaskowitz and General Friederich Wiese. Blaskowitz was an opponent of some of the Hitlerian regime's harshest tactics, while Wiese undeniably was a fervent Nazi.

Near the end of 1943, the Wehrmacht installed

an emergency fortification of 400 guns on the Mediterranean coast. Many bunkers housing the guns were camouflaged with great ingenuity. One in Antibes, flush with a handsome villa, was painted with elegant shutters and lace-curtained windows. Another sported a fake tree, flowerpots, and a false window. On the Nice waterfront, a large sign transformed a bunker into a bathhouse.

Such artistic productions failed to impress the military eye of General Blaskowitz or erase his doubts about the adequacy of his defenses. The system was too regimented; it tied down too many weapons and ammunition, and in critical spots the plan deprived his crews of necessary supply facilities. Moreover, it caused such expansion of defending divisions that they were unable to muster any kind of reserve strengths.

Estimating accurately the total military strength on the eve of the landings is difficult. It is known that Germany's two *Nineteenth Army Corps* were the forces primarily assigned for defense of areas actually attacked, and most scholars of the period accept 41,175 as the combat strength of these two units. In addition were naval and *Luftwaffe* organizations. Putting all the defending forces together, it is probable that German strength in the beaches assaulted amounted to somewhere between 285,000 and 300,000 men, but it should be remembered that one-third of this total was stationed at or near the expected invasion site of Toulon, nearly 100 miles west of the Anvil beachhead.[2]

The war had reached the stage where it was impossible to ignore American superiority in manpower and industrial muscle. Near the close of 1943, General Marshall favored invading southern France, but it was not until July of 1944 that the Combined Chiefs of Staff decided that the assault should be made by three American divisions followed by a French corps.

16

The first six months of 1944 strategists from both sides—Allied or German—worked day and night on battle plans. In their deliberations was consideration of such factors as forces available for either attacking or opposing, requests from battle commanders, terrains, statesmen, and public moods. There was not always complete harmony.

The most basic split was over long-range vision. Mark Clark stopped at Anzio kept clamoring for more troops and supplies. British participants took cues from their Prime Minister, Winston Churchill. Deeply distrustful of Soviet dictator Josef Stalin, Churchill continued to urge a drive through the Alps to Vienna or into the Balkans.

The American chiefs had little interest in pursuing Churchill's Balkan dreams and had lost enthusiasm for the campaign in Italy. General Eisenhower, Supreme

Commander of Allied forces in the European theater, endorsed a southern invasion. A Mediterranean beachhead, he argued, would erase worries of Allied forces in northern France of a possible attack on their flank. Moreover, the American government had gone to considerable expense to train and equip French divisions in North Africa, and the only way to get them into battle was through southern France.

In the middle of February, 1944, General Lucian Truscott was assigned Deputy Commander of the Sixth Corps, second in command to General Mark Clark stalled at Anzio in Italy across the Ligurian Sea.

At first light on the morning of August 15th six months later, huge formations of transport and fighter aircraft passed over the coast of southern France. Transport planes released parachutists who were followed by gliders disgorging men armed with every kind of weapon. At the same time, heavy and medium bombers were blasting beaches and coast line defenses along a twenty-five mile strip east of Toulon. Debris and smoke thickened as war ships offshore opened intense bombardment of the same terrain.

At St. Raphael and Anchor Cove in the northeast corner of St. Tropez Gulf, three American divisions—3rd, 36th, and 45th—were given the tasks of securing the beachhead as quickly as possible, then moving inland to capture the enemy's important supply bases at Le Muy and Le Luc on the Argens River valley route.

General Patch had assumed Truscott would assign his most experienced division — the 3rd Infantry Division — to his right wing where resistance was expected to be strongest, but Truscott chose the Texas National Guardsmen of the 36th Infantry Division for that task.

Ten miles inland from the St. Raphael shoreline was the town of Fréjus which Truscott viewed as critical for several reasons. The only airfield in the area was located there, and the best road inland from there followed the Argens River valley to Ly Muy before going on to Grenoble. Control of both airfield and the road would be essential to landing supplies until all major ports of the Riviera Coast were captured.

The 45th Division was to attack a beachhead near St. Maxime ten miles southwest of St. Raphael. Then the 3rd Infantry Division would be ferried over eight miles of water to go ashore at St. Tropez. Intelligence reports had warned Allied strategists that German defenders would make wide use of artillery, guns, railway artillery, French and Italian naval guns, medium and light field artillery, self-propelled guns and tanks.

Ten miles inland from the St. Raphael shoreline was the town of Fréjus, which Truscott viewed as critical for several reasons. The only airfield in the area was located there, and the best road inland from there followed the Argens River valley to Ly Muy before going on to Grenoble. Control of both airfield and the road would be essential to landing supplies until all major ports of the Riviera coast were captured. All beaches were mined and it should be expected that the Germans had enough reserve for counterattacks on whatever forces the Allies tried to land.

Admiral Hewitt's naval forces had been assigned responsibility for removal of many of the underwater obstacles to insure safer delivery of troops going ashore. Demolition teams were specialists trained to destroy by hand-placed charges and similar methods to remove many of the underwater obstacles installed by German defenders.

The navy had its own arsenal of Apex and Drone boats. The Apex boat was a landing craft which towed two others called Drones. Each Drone was loaded with ten tons or more of high explosives, and at the appropriate time the Apex boat by means of radio control would release and direct them toward the obstructions where they would explode upon contact.

Reddy Fox was a naval version of the Bangalore torpedo—a long pipe filled with explosives which when towed or pushed into position over the obstacles would detonate. Also, the navy had rocket boats or Woofus as soldiers called them. These were landing vessels equipped with heavy weapons that could be fired in salvoes or discharged simultaneously.

The D-Day plan envisaged airborne landings behind Riviera coastlines followed by seaborne delivery of some 84,000 men and 12,000 vehicles on the target beaches. Men and vehicles of the seaborne assault would carry with them a three-day supply of food, and infantrymen would have five units of fire for all weapons.

Four days later—D+4—35,000 more men, including elements from the French army, and another 8,000 vehicles were to be fed in at five-day intervals. The planners calculated that within a month the Allies could land more than 300,000 tons of arms, fuel, and equipment.[1]

In the early spring of 1944, the forces in the Mediterranean available to the Allies amounted to a British parachute brigade, an understrength French parachute regiment, an American parachute battalion, and two batteries of U.S. parachute field artillery.

Intelligence reports disclosed that German strategists had decided that if the Allies attempted a major landing in the Mediterranean, Wehrmacht defenders would retreat. Such a decision was not surprising, for German troops in Normandy were streaming back toward the Falaise Gap. The decision sealed the fate of Marseille and Toulon; both surrendered to French forces within ten days.

17

The region along the Mediterranean which Hitler's chieftains called *der Südwall* has a history of fortification dating back to the pre-Roman era. The most significant additions were around Marseille and Toulon in the eighteenth century.

In the autumn of 1943, after the Italian armistice, the German Army took over coastal defenses of these two cities. Allied planners for Dragoon knew the two seaports were vital in supplying Nazi troops with armaments, ammunition, vehicles, food, clothing, and other supplies used in modern warfare, and General Patch fully appreciated that capture of the two ports would give the Allies a sound logistical base from which a sustained drive could be launched north to link arms with whatever friendly troops were coming down from Normandy.

Notwithstanding the deadly fighting going on in

Normandy, the Germans were not ready to abandon the ports of Marseille and Toulon. On orders from *der Fuhrer* the cities were to be held "to the last man."

Air raids on Toulon began the second week of August, 1944, and were supported with overwhelming pressure from French columns in the north and east which were aided by the ever present maqui.

German resistance started to crumble like a house of cards. On August 14th the senior German officer wrote a paper declaring, "There have been too many deaths. I cannot continue." With that face-saving trail, he and more than six hundred men walked into captivity.

Forty miles west of Toulon was the great commercial harbor of Marseille, the second largest city in France. The ancient port founded by the Greeks around 600 B.C.E., contained two harbors: a rectangular Old Port (*Vieux Port*), and a huge more modern harbor to the northwest of the metropolis.

Just as at Toulon, Marseille boasted seemingly formidable defenses; on its outskirts were roadblocks and minefields as well as numerous coastal batteries and anti-submarine nets around its offshore islands, and blocking ships anchored in the harbor waiting to be sunk if the Allies attempted a landing.

Tasked with defense of Marseille was a Wehrmacht Division weakened by transfer of one of its regiments and two of its artillery batteries. The remaining formations in the Division consisted of *Volksdeutsche*—ethnic Germans from Eastern Europe—who had little enthusiasm for their assignment. The major advance on Marseille was spearheaded by the First Armored Division of French Forces and was largely unopposed because the Germans had not fortified roads leading into the city. This failure left it free for de Lattre to range his troops all around the city.

Another factor contributing to the capture of Marseille were activities by more than 500 armed Résistants, who were encouraged by reports from Paris where it was clear that days of occupation there by the Nazis were numbered.

On August 21st German tank positions on the eastern edge of Marseille were overrun in a sharp fight during which French colonial troops went in at bayonet point. According to de Lattre, the fighting was confusing and untidy: *In a few yards, one passed from the enthusiasm of a liberated boulevard into the solitude of a machine-gunned avenue. In a few turns of the track, one would meet a tank covered with flowers and carrying a smiling girl, or be fired at by an 88mm shell.*[1]

By August 25th troops of the 7th Algerian Regiment had captured the cathedral of Notre Dame de la Garde, a massive basilica which dominated the Old Port. Inside the cathedral the Algerians found a priest, some Franciscan monks, and seventy-four German soldiers seeking sanctuary from the city's vengeful civilian population. In mid-afternoon of the same day, the Algerians controlled the cathedral and the *Tricoleur* was hoisted over its bell tower.

Ten miles east of Toulon and a scant mile inward from the beach was Hyéres. Without a seaport or storage area, Hyéres was not a strategic target but a rich Riviera resort where artists, authors, retired military officers or diplomats, and emigrés lived in comfort; its capture would be little but a trophy for the Allies.

The 3rd Algerian Infantry Division consisting mainly of Moroccans was already positioned between Marseille and Toulon. These forces known as goumiers were indigenous Muslim soldiers who served in auxiliary units of the French Army of Africa between 1908 and 1956. Normally under service to the State of Morocco, goumiers served under command of French officers and were included as parts of the Free French Forces (FFR).

Goumier units were assigned to liberate Hyéres. The Algerian Division's tripartite standard reflected its cultural heritage—red, white, red—with three waning crescent moons of blue, white, and red arranged in the center band.

As soon as they had touched French soil, the Moroccans were sent into battle. By nightfall of the first day they were at the gates of Aubagne northeast of Marseille; the road to Hyéres was wide open.

Algerian goumiers were colorful, not just for the mules that carried supplies but also for the practice of wearing the ears of foes overcome in combat. Attired in striped *djellabas* and with boots hanging around their necks, goumiers marched into Hyéres where crowds gathered, cheered, and offered flowers. The paraders sang in French a North African anthem: "*It is we the Africans who have come from afar.*"

Cheering spectators automatically responded with "*La Marseillaise.*"

The Division commander of German forces charged with defense of Marseille was Lieutenant General Hans Schaefer, a veteran of the Eastern Front, who had been badly wounded near Kharkov a year earlier. Upon recovery and a very short rehab, he had returned to active duty in April 1944, and been assigned to defend Marseille.

Schaefer was pessimistic about the ability of Marseille to withstand an assault. He overestimated the numbers of Résistants, guessing there must have been more than 50,000 of them. Later Intelligence would show there were only about 500 armed activists.

While German positions north and south of Marseille were being mopped up one by one, Schaefer, increasingly isolated, held on. He agreed to see opposition leaders and arrangements were made to permit them to cross defense perimeters for a meeting behind German lines.

The meeting was unproductive. Schaefer ranted

about Résistants, whose actions he argued had caused *Vieux Port* to become a combat area and thus a target for German artillery fire from the harbor's ports. The gathering closed. Algerian leaders were allowed to return through the lines back to their own quarters, and the battle continued.

French military leaders positioned their units around the eastern and northern outskirts of the city within five miles of its heart and settled down to wait for reinforcements. One battalion of the Algerian *Trailleurs*, however, kept getting calls from activists inside Marseille. These calls, along with the crowds of exuberant French citizens, moved a unit of the *Trailleurs* into action.

In the early hours of August 23rd the battalion plunged into the city itself. By 8 o'clock that morning, the battalion was cutting through the center of Marseille and at its waterfront. The rest of the regiment was able to come down from the north and northeast. That unplanned drive decided the issue, and fighting became a matter of battling street to street, house to house, and from one strongpoint to the next with ever-increasing help from ardent, supporting citizens.[2]

On August 28th the same day as the capitulation at Toulon, General Hans Schaefer amassed his forces at Marseille. The French had lost 1,825 men killed or wounded in the battle for Marseille and had taken 11,000 prisoners.

18

In June of 1944, General Jacob Devers, Director of North Africa Theater of Operations, named Major General Robert T. Frederick commander of this disparate coagulation. At the time, there was little to distinguish Frederick from his classmates.

Cadet Robert Frederick graduated from West Point, standing 124th in a class of 250, and immediately went on active duty in artillery branch where he gained experience in harbor defenses and antiaircraft weapons. Many of his early duty stints lay outside the usual parameters of military training. As a lieutenant colonel he requested assignment to the U.S. Army's Special Forces, and in this branch trained for commando-type missions in winter and mountain warfare. Other assignments would catch the attention of Generals Marshall and Eisenhower, so Frederick rose in rank rapidly. By February 1944, he had reached that of brigadier general.

Churchill once called Frederick "the greatest fighting general of all time," and Germans referred to him as *Schwartzer Teufel*—Black Devil. He was the only U. S. serviceman to receive eight Purple Hearts that earned him the moniker "the most shot-at-and-hit general in American history."

Frederick was a colonel when he volunteered for the First Special Service Force. Becoming leader of the joint American-Canadian brigade, he supervised its training in Montana and was at its head while in Alaska and later in pitched battles against the Nazis in Italy, including the fighting at Anzio.

By January 1944, Frederick's forces had been given the sobriquet Devils Brigade after a diary found on a dead German soldier which read: "The Black Devils are all around us. We never hear them come." It was a reference to the silent, deadly night raids conducted by Frederick's men who left behind them a trail of sentries with throats slit.

Frederick was not in the swashbuckling George Patton mold. A 1928 West Point graduate, he was midway in class standing, but recognized for dedication as much as Ulysses S. Grant or George Patton. Mild mannered and mustachioed, Frederick looked like the leading man in a Hollywood film.

Frederick was an oddball—rumors were that he had made his first parachute jump wearing bedroom slippers, and others asserted that in combat the only things he carried with him were his rifle, Nescafe, cigarettes, and a letter in Latin from a Catholic bishop that commended him "as absolutely worthy of trust."

Frederick was in the back seat of a half-track nearing Rome and was crossing a bridge over the Tiber when his driver was killed by a German sniper, whose shots also hit Frederick.

Frederick's career earned him two Distinguished Service Crosses, and it was said that his men worshipped him because he shared their hardships and never blamed them if things went wrong. Many veterans of the Devils Brigade said that they would have followed him to hell and back if he had asked them.

Frederick was told Intelligence reports disclosed that German strategists had decided that if the Allies launched a major landing in the Mediterranean, Wehrmacht defenders would retreat. Such a decision was not surprising because German troops in Normandy were streaming back toward the Falaise Gap. The decision sealed the fate of Marseille and Toulon in the Mediterranean area; both surrendered to French forces within ten days.

General Truscott was generous in his praise of Frederick writing that "Frederick's feat in organizing, training, and leading this composite force in battle was one of the most remarkable airborne drops of the war."[1]

Frederick's mission was to drop his airborne troops in the Argens valley near Le Muy in order to block roads leading back to the beachhead landing and then attack Fréjus from the rear.

19

Offshore and aboard the command ship *Catoctin*, General Patch continued studying maps of the Riviera and contemplating his actions. His first objective had been to secure the landing area by seizing the ports of Toulon and Marseille. Control of those would give him a logistical base necessary for troops which once ashore would be driving north to join whatever Allied forces were coming down from northern France. That objective had been achieved, and he had created the Butler Task Force with Lucian Truscott to head its penetration of the Argens Valley.

The Task Force with its motorized infantry battalion, its thirty medium tanks, twelve tank destroyers, twelve self-propelled artillery pieces, armored cars, light tanks and trucks of the cavalry squadron constituted a balanced, mobile offensive unit.

Four days after landing near St. Raphael, the Butler

Task Force was well on its way north and was approaching Sisteron. Patch radioed Truscott to alert one infantry division to prepare for a drive on to Grenoble. After receiving that message, Truscott in turn radioed Butler, instructing him to hold at Sisteron and await reinforcements. However, if feasible he should continue to send patrols westward to determine the practicability of seizing the high ground just north of Montélimar, a small city on the east bank of the Rhone River. The city was sixty miles west of Sisteron and lay astride the most probable German route of withdrawal.

Even after reaching Sisteron, Butler still considered Grenoble his primary objective and responded to Truscott's message that he would carry out the reconnaissance but warned that he was running short of fuel and supplies. He further requested firm orders as to whether Grenoble to the north was still to be his main objective or should he move toward Montélimar to the west.

Truscott, now confident that Allied air superiority ruled out any possible counterattack, conferred with General Patch and the two of them decided that Butler's next objective should be capture of Montélimar.

It was 2045 on August 20th before a radio message from Truscott made it clear. Butler was to move toward Montélimar at dawn and with all possible speed. He was to seize the town and block all routes available for

German withdrawal. The 36th Division was being ordered to come to bolster the Task Force as soon as possible.

This change of orders brought up several problems. First, commanders of the 36th Division had yet to be informed of the switch in the main effort from Grenoble to Montélimar. Secondly, Butler's advance had been achieved while he was oriented toward Grenoble, and the change demanded time to reassemble his scattered forces. At the same time, Truscott's order made it clear no matter how stiff the opposition he was to hold his position until 36th Division units could arrive.

Butler was still unsure of the enemy's strength and dispositions in the immediate area, and now his Task Force was spread out over approximately ninety miles of rough, mountainous terrain. He had assigned most of his heavy weapons to blocking two major passes threatened by German formations operating from Grenoble.

Butler realized he was at the end of a 235-mile supply chain, and he had learned that Truscott's three Divisions consumed 100,000 gallons of fuel a day. The Task Force had been allotted only 1,000 gallons for the beachhead landing although these were augmented somewhat by 25,000 gallons of captured stock.

The town of Montélimar lies on a flat plain along the north bank of the Rubion River, and about sixteen miles northeast of Montélimar is the village of Puy St.

Martin. German forces had begun traveling north along the main highway and Butler ordered his men to open fire on them. A second battery and several tanks and tank destroyers arrived to join his troops while a cavalry troop and more infantry put up a roadblock across the highway. The block lasted until a German reprisal at dusk drove the Task Force attackers back into the hills.[1]

Despite occasional minor successes, German forces at this stage of the withdrawal were disorderly rather than determined. A local priest disparaged them in his memoirs by writing: *German columns continually passing. They have more and more the appearance of hunted beasts… Tanks help them get through the Resistance. They get Frenchmen and place them on the hoods of their cars…. This afternoon they took some young people and used them as shields.*[2]

20

Early in 1943, the occupying Germans had decided to destroy the Old Port of Marseilles and rid it of resistant inhabitants. An estimated 25,000 citizens were given orders to leave the city within 48 hours. A fifth of them were permitted to depart freely, the remainder sent to Fréjus in cattle cars. Jews were transported to special camps, and others sought refuge with family or friends. Then the Germans proceeded to blow up acres of buildings, leaving the historic center of Marseille in ruins.

Heavy coastal batteries and rail spurs were built specifically to handle railroad guns with barrels up to 15 inches in diameter. Offshore minefields, boom nets, and submarine detectors were complemented by block ships anchored at strategic places to be sunk on a moment's notice.

Marseilles' defense forces were led by *Generalmajor*

Hans Schaefer, who had been returned to duty after being badly wounded on the Russian front. He was expected to hold on to Marseille but had no air cover or naval or ground support.

Having just arrived in March, 1944, Shaefer had no real understanding of the civil unrest in Marseille. Probably the FFI (Free Forces of the Interior) numbered less than 1,000 men and women at the time, but worsening economic conditions soon swelled their ranks. Demonstrations, strikes, and occupation of factories by workers all increased.

American military chiefs had agreed that it would be most appropriate for French troops to lead the assault on Marseille and Toulon. The major advance on Marseille was spearheaded by French Army B under command of General Jean de Lattre de Tassigny.

Before sending his troops into action, de Lattre had planned to take Marseille and Toulon in succession, but the acceleration of other French landings allowed him to envision almost concurrent actions against both ports. He handed the assignment of liberating Marseille to a subordinate general who commanded the 3rd Algerian Infantry Division already positioned between Marseille and Toulon.

Taking note that the Germans, although thorough in fortifying the beachheads, were not defending the roadways leading to the two ports. The Allies had gained air supremacy, and with that assuring protection, French generals decided to land troops by parachutes, gliders, and other means north of the Durance River and then advance on Marseille and Toulon from the north and northeast.

Assault on Marseille began amidst stifling heat on the 22nd of August, and German guns were once again effective, but by noon of that day tanks had rumbled down from the north to overcome scanty obstacles and had reached the city's biggest church; attackers resorted to their bayonets.

With the aid of an intrepid priest who was an intelligence officer for the Algerians, a meeting with Generalmajor Shafer was arranged. Shafer held out against surrender, alleging that French invaders had taken sanctuary in a basilica and from there were firing at his soldiers. The commanding French general did not agree and insisted that the perpetrators could only be maquis or members of the Resistants and beyond his control.

The next morning tanks and infantry from North Africa entered the city and paraded down its main thoroughfare while citizens cheered and offered small flags, flowers, bottles of wine, and various souvenirs.

French military losses at Marseille numbered 1400 killed or wounded, almost half of whom were Moroccan recruits, plus 200 civilians. The Germans suffered 5,500 killed, a quarter of their defending forces, and another 7,000 taken prisoner. The First Armored Division of French Forces was largely unopposed because the Germans had not fortified roads leading into the city. This failure left it free for de Lattre to range his troops all around both Marseille and Toulon.

Other factors contributing to the fall of the two ports included activities by more than 500 armed Résistants, who were encouraged by reports from Paris where it was clear that days of occupation there by the Nazis were numbered.

On August 21st German tank positions on the eastern edge of Marseille were overrun in a sharp fight during which French colonial troops went in at bayonet point. By August 25th troops of the 7th Algerian Regiment had captured the cathedral of Notre Dame de la Garde, a massive basilica which dominated the Old Port. Inside the cathedral the Algerians found a priest, some Franciscan monks, and seventy-four German soldiers seeking sanctuary from the city's vengeful civilian population. In mid-afternoon of the same day, the Algerians controlled the cathedral and the *Tricoleur* was hoisted over its bell tower.

The division commander of German forces charged with defense of Marseille was Lieutenant General Hans Schaefer, a veteran of the Eastern Front, who had been badly wounded near Kharkov a year earlier. Upon recovery and very short rehabilitation, he had been returned to active duty in April 1944 and assigned to the defense of Marseille.

Schaefer was pessimistic about the ability of Marseille to withstand an assault. He overestimated the numbers of Résistants, guessing there must have been more than 50,000 of them. Later Intelligence would show there were only about 500 armed activists.

While German positions north and south of Marseille were being mopped up one by one, Schaefer, increasingly isolated, held on. He agreed to see opposition leaders, and arrangements were made to permit them to cross defense perimeters for a meeting behind German lines.

The meeting was unproductive. Schaefer ranted about Résistants, whose actions he argued had caused *Vieux Port* to become a combat area and thus a target for German artillery fire from the harbor's ports. The gathering closed, Algerian leaders were allowed to return through the lines back to their own quarters, and the battle continued.

French military leaders positioned their units around the eastern and northern outskirts of the city within five miles of its heart and settled down to wait for reinforcements. One battalion of the Algerian *Trailleurs*, however, kept getting calls from activists inside Marseille. These calls along with the crowds of exuberant French citizens moved a unit of the *Trailleurs* into action.

In the early hours of August 23rd the battalion plunged into the city itself. By 8 o'clock that morning the battalion was cutting through the center of Marseille and at its waterfront. The rest of the regiment was able to come down from the north and northeast. That unplanned drive decided the issue, and fighting became a matter of battling street to street, house to house, and from one strongpoint to the next with ever-increasing help from ardent, supporting citizens.[1]

On August 28th the same day as the capitulation at Toulon, General Hans Schaefer surrendered his forces at Marseille. The French had lost 1,825 men killed or wounded in the battle for Marseille and had taken 11,000 prisoners.

21

Weighing accurately the overall effect of French and Algerian forces in helping win Southern France, including battles from Marseille east to beyond St. Raphael is no precise matter. Casualty reports from de Lattre's Army B range from 933 to 1,513 combatants killed and from 3,732 to 5,393 wounded. Figures from the other side show approximately 35,000 prisoners, including 700 officers, with estimates of German dead hovering around 5,500.

The strategy adopted by the Allies in taking Marseille and Toulon was commended by the Chief of Staff for the 19th German Army, *Generallieutenant* Walter Bosch, who wrote:

> The defense of the ports was planned by the German Navy on the basis of a frontal attack and so almost all the batteries (they were the best batteries) were

concentrated in the vicinity of the ports, and others were behind embrasures and emplaced in such a way that they could fire only toward the sea and a small sector of land. Thus it happened that most of the coastal batteries fired not a single shot, either during the landing itself or during the struggle for the harbors of Marseille and Toulon. [1]

The Seventh Army's race up the Rhone was confronted by the difficult terrain of the Vosges Mountains — a much easier defensive position for the beleaguered *German Nineteenth Army*, which could no longer trade space for time to organize opposition. Indeed, the *Nineteenth* was on the ropes; more than 1,000 of its men had been taken prisoners, and by the beginning of September 1944 even its formidable Panzer units had sustained significant losses.

Yet not all was rosy for the Allies. They, too, were showing signs of fatigue. Casualties, light at first, had begun to mount, and logistic problems were limiting advances of the infantry. The VI Corps listed 2,050 killed, captured, or missing out of a total 9,900 casualties. The French record was even darker, for in the heavy fighting around Marseille and Toulon the lightly armed FFI paid heavily for the gain of every yard.

On August 17th 1944, American General Patch repeated his previous order to General Truscott that he was to leave Marseille and Toulon to the French and continue moving to the north and west. As the month closed, fighting around Montélimar had come to a boil.

Allied Intelligence informed General Patch that the Germans intended to regroup their forces around Dijon, some two hundred miles north of Montélimar, and planned to employ the 11th Panzer Division to shield forces then retreating to the east of the Rhone. Truscott's 6th Corps was to maintain pursuing them to Lyon, France's third city, and then on to Dijon.

The primary objectives of Allied advances up the Rhone Valley were to unite with and join General George Patton's Third Army now sweeping across France from Normandy toward Germany. The sweep was expected to capture large numbers of Wehrmacht troops, thus decimating the Reich's military commands fleeing southward. The driving force for the operation during this transitional period would be the brigade-sized unit led by General Frederick B. Butler.

Butler's Task Force included Sherman tanks and tank destroyers, motorized infantry, field artillery, a reconnaissance squadron, plus support outfits—3,000 troops and 1,000 vehicles in all.

Early on the morning of August 18th, Butler moved his forces away from the landing area and forward due north toward Digne and Gap. Digne was located at an intersection by which the Germans could bring reinforcements from Italy. Arrival of American armored squadron so soon clearly surprised Wehrmacht generals who must have been thinking of the slow breakout underway in Normandy.

By August 15th, Butler's Task Force was approaching Sisteron. Four days later, General Patch instructed General Truscott to prepare an infantry division to take Grenoble and also ordered Butler to remain at Sisteron and await reinforcements. Perhaps with the failure of Clark to take the high ground at Anzio, Truscott urged Butler to consider the advantages of seizing the high terrain just north of Montélimar, this small town on the east banks of the Rhone just 60 miles west of Sisteron and only 50 miles north of the important city of Avignon.

Radio communications between Truscott and Butler had become increasingly ragged, and the only message that Butler could ascertain was that his Task Force's mission remained unchanged; Grenoble was still his primary objective.

American priorities shifted and decisions by Patch and Truscott resulted in orders that Butler was to hold to the capture of Montélimar and block any withdrawal of the German 19th Army. As soon as reinforcements arrived, Task Force Butler would be attached to the 36th Division and under its command.

Clarity of a sort had come, but Butler's situation

was not enviable. His forces were spread over more than ninety miles of rough, mountainous terrain; most of his heavy weapons had been assigned to Allied forces blocking two major mountainous passes threatened by enemy formations operating from Grenoble, and he was at the end of a 235-mile chain expending ammunition, artillery and tank rounds at an alarming rate.

For men in the oncoming 36th Division, the journey to Montélimar made at night through narrow, winding, rain-swept country roads in German-held territory must have been exhausting and dangerous. One officer in the Division, Major Marcel F. Pinzetl recalled an episode:

> It was night and we were moving forward under blackout conditions. We followed the noise of the tank treads ahead as it was too dark to see. When dawn came we found to our surprise that our jeep had been following a German tank. The tank noticed us and also stopped. We were lightly armed so we turned off the road and the jeep turned over on its side ... We ran for cover. The tank backed up; the hatch opened, and the gunner took aim. Then one German soldier got out of the tank and walked over to our jeep, took out his knife and cut the rope holding the wheel of cheese we had liberated, and took it to the tank and left.[2]

22

General Truscott assigned the 3rd Infantry Division to land on the westernmost beaches just to the southwest of St. Tropez where planners expected to face the toughest German counterattacks. Landing in that area would place the 3rd Division close to the primary ports of Marseille and Toulon and be in a position to protect the flank of the French II Corps.

Early on August 16, the Division began its assault to the west. After all of its assault units were ashore, the 3rd Division began its push further inland, and by dusk of the next day three of the Division's Regiments had broken through the heavily wooded, steep mountainous region just beyond their landing beaches. The infantry encountered some small arms fire, but the main threat was the abundant German artillery fire, although it was not especially accurate due to a lack of forward observers.

St. Raphael fell to the 143rd Infantry in the morning of August 16th and in the afternoon of the same day the 141st Division captured neighboring Theoule-sur-Mer. With those gains, the Division prepared to move toward the northwest.

Battalions of the 157th and the 180th landed and started to drive toward Vidauban, Le Luc, and Les Arcs. By the morning of August 17th both communities were in American hands, and when that evening came, Butler had assembled his Task Force just north of Le Muy.

The Division's reserve regiment, the 179th, also had landed and was now able to bolster more aid for the invaders. All the Allied forces were ashore and ready to move inland. Armed invaders aided by maquis had overcome defenders and were now ready to exploit a weak and confused enemy.

Total casualties for the entire 45th Infantry Division were two officers and a hundred and seven enlisted men — all killed in action.

The next day the main body of the Task Force struck out northwest, crossing to the west bank of the Durance River to take advantage of better roads and continue its drive toward Sisteron. The only significant action took place at Digne, 15 miles southeast of Sisteron, where the Task Force helped by maquis and FFI overcame 500 defenders — mainly administrative units — to surrender after several hours of fighting.[1]

At *Oberkommando der Wehrmacht* (OKW) headquarters there was more concern about northern France than happenings in the southern parts of the divided country. The Allied breakout from Normandy beachheads at St. Lo, failure of the German counterattack at Mortain, and threatened Allied envelopment of German forces in the Falaise Pocket—all pointed toward disaster for the Reich.

Complicating challenges for the defenders were conflicting orders and poor communications. It was noon on August 18th before General Blaskowitz, Commander of Army Group G and General Fredrich Wiese, heading the Nineteenth Army, received orders to withdraw northward from the positions they were attempting to hold.

The garrisons at Marseille and Toulon were ordered by Hitler to fight to the last death. As the third week of August began, the appearance of American mechanized troops north of the Durance River was an unwelcome surprise, and General Fredrich Wiese, Commander of the Nineteenth Army, concluded that his problem now was to establish lines that would give his forces west of the Rhone River the ability to cross to its east banks where they could set up stronger defenses or possibly launch a counter offensive operation. The rapid advance westward soon made such plans obsolete.

French forces were pressing for the capitulation of

Toulon, and while fighting there was still going on, German defenses to its east lost cohesion and began crumbling. Negotiations were opened for surrender of beleaguered German troops.

The last organized resistance at Toulon ended on August 26th and the defending troops there surrendered two days later. The battle cost the French about 2,700 men killed or wounded, while the Germans lost their entire garrison of 18,000 men. The French claimed, however, to have taken more than 17,000 prisoners, indicating that only about a thousand Germans had given their lives in defending the port—hardly a good attempt to follow Hitler's order to fight until the last man.

Far off to the north, the mood in German Headquarters was gloomy. Minister of Propaganda Josef Goebbels voiced a warning that was read over Radio Berlin: "We must be prepared for a German withdrawal from France. We should expect the loss of places with world-famous names."

Among those unspoken places were the Mediterranean cities of Nice, Cannes, Marseille, and Toulon. *Volkischer Beobachter*, the Nazi Party's newspaper, printed, "It is out of the question to send reinforcements to France."

Of the sixty divisions Hitler had in western Europe, fifteen had been destroyed, fifteen others badly mauled, and the rest were in peril, most notably those under the command of General Blaskowitz's Army Group in southern France. In the embattled zones, French patriots were rising to fight the Boche, to serve as guides for the attacking Allied forces, and to provide crucial information to American and British airplanes which wiped out bridges, paralyzed enemy camps, and pounded withdrawal routes for the retreating Germans.

At his headquarters in a villa just outside St. Tropez, General Lucian Truscott weighed the record of Operation Dragoon. So far, everything looked good. Frederick's paratroopers and glidermen had seized their objectives and were in control of land marked off by a semi-circled Blue Line extending from shores near Cape Negre to rise and reach beaches ten miles northeast of St. Raphael.

Truscott focused his attention on maps of the Rhone Valley and on routes his Seventh Army might take to link up General George Patton's Third Army which Intelligence had informed him was driving rapidly from Normandy toward Germany.

23

German intelligence reports convinced General Wiese, Nineteenth Army Commander, that Allied forces above Montélimar posed a serious obstacle to his northward withdrawal. He responded by ordering his most powerful and most mobile force, the 11th Panzer Division, to come and buttress the troubled area. The order though was hard to execute, for fuel shortages and the difficulty of marching at night delayed the Panzer Division's movement. Not until dawn on August 23rd could Panzer reinforcements be brought into play at Montélimar.

North of Montélimar, the 143rd Infantry had captured Grenoble before moving farther to stop at Valence twenty miles north of the Drome River. General Truscott next ordered Butler to move his men across the Drome and close all its crossing sites. To Truscott's disappointment, vigorous fighting continued, and the primary objective of his maneuver was inconclusive.

Germans again had frustrated American attempts to cut their withdrawal route, and losses in men and materiel continued to multiply. As long as they could, German soldiers continued to flee over the Drome River in ones and twos and disorganized groups. The battle for the area officially ended on August 31st when the American 142nd Infantry Regiment reached the Rhone River, clearing the north bank of the Drome and taking more than 650 German prisoners.

Although exhausted and disorganized, General Wiese's Nineteenth Army had managed to save the bulk of the 11th Panzer Division. The battle for southernmost France was over, and a race for the German border was next.

Despite heavy German losses in personnel and equipment, the escape of the Nineteenth Army was a disappointment for General Truscott. From the outset, the oblique advance of the Grenoble-Montélimar area had been a gamble. The failure of General Wiese to protect the flanks of his hasty withdrawal had been a godsend for American troops. Moreover, assistance from the FFI in harassing retreating Germans, supplying valuable local intelligence to the advancing Americans, and boosting their combat forces wherever possible, were Allied assets often overlooked.

The primary objectives of troops advancing northward up the Rhone Valley were to join up with General

ASSAULTING THE RIVIERA, 1944

George Patton's Third Army sweeping across France from Normandy toward Germany. Weeks of mud, field rations, and heavy fighting paid off when handshakes between men of the Third Army and those in the Seventh Army coming from the south gave the Allies a broad front from Switzerland to the English Channel. Yet all was not rosy for Allied strategists. Patton's Army largely unopposed had marched through France but had been halted at Metz. The Seventh Army's race up the Rhone Valley had reached the difficult terrain of the Vosges Mountains—a much easier defensive position for Germany's beleaguered Nineteenth Army. Logistics problems had forced the infantry to advance on foot, and casualties, light at first, had begun to mount. The VI Corps had lost more than 2,000 killed, captured or missing; French troops had lost even more in heavy fighting around Marseille and Toulon, and lightly armed volunteers in the FFI had sacrificed in unrecorded numbers.

Added to losses in manpower was the increasingly bad weather bringing rain and cold, swollen rivers, and trench foot. Also contributing to temporary confusion and misunderstandings among the disparate Allied forces was a shift in the chain of command. Control of Allied troops in the Mediterranean was assigned to SHAEF where American General Dwight D. Eisenhower was Supreme Commander.

In August of 1944, Eisenhower chose Lieutenant

General Jacob Devers to be Commanding General of the Sixth Army Group, giving him control of the U. S. Seventh Army and French First armies in the Mediterranean after landings were made on the Riviera.

As September began, General Eisenhower at SHAEF drew up several missions for General Jacob Devers, a general wearing many hats, the most recent as Lieutenant General commanding the Sixth Army Group. Assignments given to Devers were: 1) protect the southern flank of the 12th Army Group, 2) destroy the enemy west of the Rhine, 3) secure the river crossings, and 4) breach the Siegfried Line.[1]

Devers and Patch visited Truscott, leader of the VI Corps and told him there would be almost no reserves to back up the light resistance they expected him to encounter in his advance toward Strasbourg.[2]

The two explained their plans to advance toward Strasboug on the west bank of the Rhine via the pass at St. Die and the compromise they had made with French Generals Charles de Gaulle and Philippe LeClerc to hold American forces outside Strasbourg and let French troops enter and liberate the city.

Philippe Francois Marie LeClerc was the son of an aristocratic family and when a young adult went to the French Military Academy, graduating from there in 1924. During the 2nd World War he fought in the Battle of France and became one of the first to make his way to Britain to fight with the Free French under the leadership of General Charles de Gaulle.

LeClerc led raids in the Italian-controlled Libya and after his forces had captured Kufra he had his men swear an oath known as *sement de Koufra* in which they pledged to fight until their flag flew over the Strasbourg Cathedral.

From November 20th, 21st, and 22nd Allied infantry slugged a path from the northeast before halting at Saverne. The Saverne "gap" is the historic gateway through the barrier of the Vosges Mountains opening a line to Strasbourg.

Strasbourg had been the focus of French-German enmity since the Franco-Prussian War of 1870-1871, and Generals Patch and Truscott recommended to Supreme Allied Headquarters that French forces be primary in recapturing the city. Accordingly, American troops were halted at the Saverne "gap" forty kilometers northwest of Strasbourg to allow units of the French 2nd Armored Division under Philippe LeClerc be first to enter the city. The FFI led by LeClerc entered the city on November 23rd and by 2:30 that afternoon the French Tricolor flew over the Strasbourg cathedral.

The rapid liberation of Strasbourg by LeClerc's 2nd Armor Division set off a torrent of joy throughout France, representing a victory for the Western Allies and a symbolic win for French citizens.

German accounts of Strasbourg's capture are bleak, describing the capture as an "inglorious episode" in German military history. The SS had looted Strasbourg before withdrawing, and soldiers ordered to "fight to the last round" chose instead to throw away their equipment and surrender. The Wehrmacht defense in this instance was blamed as being premature and ignominious.

Though the invasion was controversial, there were two undeniable positives. First, it returned France to self-government. Having been defeated in a *blitzkrieg* lasting only six weeks in 1940, their government in exile and having no political or military voice, the successes of the French First Army provided a national fillip and pride. The FFI (*Forces Françaises de l'Intérieur*)—a mixture of the Résistance and ex-service men—flocked to the banner as France was liberated.

A second and more strategically important benefit was recapturing control of Marseille, a vital port for delivery of nearly all war materiél for all Allied forces. The Germans had tried to stop Marseille from being so used, but the efficiency of U.S. Army and U.S. Navy salvage teams restored the facilities and had the port running by late September, 1944.

There was still much to be done before the Third Reich, one that its *Fuhrer* had promised would last a thousand years, ended. Yet giant strides had been taken by a conglomerate of Allies. Before another year had passed, its leader was a burned skeleton in a Berlin bunker.

War in Europe ended in May, 1945, and terrible fighting lay ahead in the Pacific. Yet united efforts by U.S. citizens and scientists merged with the unlimited courage of its men and women, the feckless Japanese venture at Pearl Harbor was fully vindicated in August of 1945.

BIBLIOGRAPHY

Blumenson, Martin. Mark Clark: *Last of the Great WWII Commanders*. New York: Gordon & Weed, 1984.

Breuer, William B. *Operation Dragoon: Allied Invasion of Southern France*. New York: Jove Books, 1988.

Churchill, Winston S. *Triumph and Tragedy*. Boston: Houghton- Mifflin, 1953.

Clark, Mark W. *Calculated Risk*. New York: Enigma Books, 1950, p. 180.

Clarke, Jeffrey J. and Robert Ross Smith, eds. *Riviera to the Rhine*. Washington, D.C.: Center of Military History, United States Army, 1993.

Connole, Dennis A. *A "Yankee" in the "Texas"Army*. London: Brassey's, 2008.

Craven, W. F. and J. L. Cate. *The Army Air Forces in WWII*. Vols. II and III. University of Chicago Press, Chicago, Illinois, 1949.

Cross, Robin. *Operation Dragoon*. New York: Pegasus Books, 2019. Eisenhower, Dwight D. *Crusade in Europe*. New York: Doubleday & Company, 1951.

Forty, Simon. *From the Riviera to the Rhine*. Philadelphia: Casemate Publishers, 2018.

Freidel, Frank. *Franklin D. Roosevelt: A Rendezvous with Destiny*. Boston: Little Brown, and Company, 1990.

Funk, Arthur Layton. *Hidden Ally: The French Resistance, Special Operations and the Landings in Southern France, 1944*. New York: Greenwood Press, 1992.

Gassend, Jean-Loup. *Operation Dragoon: Autopsy of a Battle* (Allied Liberation of Southern France). Atglen, P.A. Schiffler Publishing, 2014.

Hodgson, James. *Army Combat Journal*. Washington, D.C., 1954.

Kundahl, George G. The Riviera at War. New York: I. B. Tauris, 2017.

Manchester, William. *The Glory and the Dream*. New York: Bantam Books, 1975.

Mazower, Mark. *Hitler's Empire, Nazi Rule in Occupied Europe*. London: Allen Lane, 2008.

Moore, William Mortimer. *Free France's Lion: The Life of Philippe LeClerc, De Gaulle's Greatest General*. Newbury, Nerkshire: Casemate Publishers, 2011.

Morison, Samuel Eliot. *The Oxford History of the American People*. New York: Oxford University Press, 1965.

Murphy, Audie. *To Hell and Back*. New York: Henry Holt and Company, 2002.

Morris, Richard B. *Encyclopedia of American History*. New York: Harper & Brothers, 1953.

O'Reilly, Bill and Martin Dugard. *Killing Patton*. New York: Henry Holt and Company, LLC, 2014.

Pogue, Forest C. *The Supreme Command*. U.S. Army in WWII.

European Theater of Operations. Washington, D.C. Center of Military History, 1986.

Potter, E.B. and Chester W. Nimitz. *Sea Power*. Englewood Cliffs, N.J: Prentice Hall, 1960.

Ricks, Thomas E. *The Generals*. New York: The Penguin Press, 2012.

Truscott, Lucian K. *Command Missions*. New York: N.Y. E. P. Dutton and Company, 2017.

Tucker-Jones, Anthony. *Operation Dragoon: The Liberation of Southern France 1944*. Pen and Sword, ISBN 978-1-84884-140-6.

Yeide, Harry and Mark Stout. *First to the Rhine*. St. Paul, MN: Zenith Press, 2007.

ENDNOTES

Chapter 2

1. Winston Churchill, Their Finest Hour, pp.74-118. Boston: Houghton Mifflin 1949. See also B. H. Liddell Hart, *History of the Second World War*, pp. 79-80. London: Cassell, 1970.
2. *New York Times*, August 18, 1940.

Chapter 5

1. As quoted by Thomas E. Ricks. *The Generals*. New York: The Penguin Press, 2012. P. 55.

Chapter 7

1. Harry Yeide and Mark Stout. *First to the Rhine*. St. Paul, Mn.: Zenith Press, 2007. Pp. 13-14.
2. Anthony Tucker-Jones, *Operation Dragoon: The Liberation of Southern France 1944*. Penand Sword. P. 11.

3. Breuer, *op. cit.*, p. 244.
4. William K. Wyant. T*he Story of the Century: A Biography of Lt. General Alexander M. Patch.* SanFrancisco, California: Praeger Press, 1991. P. 244.
5. Pogue, *op. cit.*, p. 2.
6. E. B. Potter and Chester W. Nimitz. *Sea Power.* Engelwood Cliffs, N.J: Prentice Hall,1960. Pp. 588-98.

Chapter 8

1. Yeide and Stout, *op. cit.*, pp.16-17.
2. Clarke, Jeffrey J. and Robert Ross Smith. *Riviera to the Rhine.* Minnetonka, MN: National Historical Society, 1995. Pp. 41-43.
3. As quoted in Yeide and Stout. *op. cit*, p. 39.Chapter Nine Wyant, *op. cit.* P. 210.

Chapter 10

1. Churchill, Winston S. *Triumph and Tragedy.* Boston: Houghton-Mifflin, 1953. Pp. 94-95.
2. Yeide and Stout. *op. cit.*, pp. 12-15.
3. Clark, Mark W. *Calculated Risk.* New York: Enigma Books, 1950, p. 180.
4. As quoted by Ricks, Thomas E. *The Generals.* New York: Penguin Press, 2012. P. 66.
5. Blumenson, *op. cit.*, p. 131.
6. As quoted in Morison, *op. cit.*, p. 1022.

Chapter 11

1. Pogue, *op. cit.*, p. 227.
2. Breuer, *op. cit.*, p. 46.

Chapter 12

1. Truscott, *Command Missions*, p. 440.
2. Yeide and Stout. *op. cit.*, P. 97.

Chapter 13

1. Clarke and Smith, *op. cit.*, pp. 154-160.
2. As told in Yeide & Stout, *op.cit.*, pp. 5051
3. Audie Murphy, July 1945, Audie Murphy Research Foundation Newspaper. Vol. 4, Spring 1948.
4. Yeide and Stout. *op. cit.*, P. 97.

Chapter 14

1. Jacob L. Devers. "Operation Dragoon: Invasion of Southern France." *Military Affairs*, Summer, 1946, 2-41.

Chapter 15

1. Breuer, *op. cit.*, pp. 48-49.

2. Hodgson, James. "Counting Combat Noses," *Army Combat Journal*. Vol. 5. No. 2, September, 1954, pp. 45-46.

Chapter 16

1. Robin Cross. *Operation Dragoon*. New York: Pegasus Books, 2019. Pp. 96-97.

Chapter 17

1. As quoted in Cross, *op, cit., p. 236.*
2. Clarke and Smith. *River to the Rhine, pp. 140–42.*

Chapter 18

1. Truscott, Lucian K. *Command Decisions*. New York: E. P. Dutton and Company, 2017. Pp. 430-31.

Chapter 19

1. Clarke and Smith, *op. cit.*, p. 149.
2. Cross, *op. cit.*, p. 202.

Chapter 20

1. As quoted by Cross, *p. 236.*

Chapter 21

1. *Generallieutenant* Walter Bosch, *"Critique of the American Seventh Army,"* William Quinn Papers, MilitaryHistory Institute, Boxes 19 and 5, Heritage Trust Library, Washington, D.C.
2. Dennis A. Connole, *A "Yankee" in the "Texas Army,* London: Brassey's, 2008.

Chapter 22

1. Clarke and Smith. *Riviera to the Rhine.* Pp. 128-133.

Chapter 23

1. Yeide and Stout, *op. cit.*, p. 192. Also see Truscott, *op. cit.*, p. 445.

ACKNOWLEDGEMENTS

An author anxious for publication is somewhat like an expectant father awaiting his first child. The impatience of a writer to see his words in book form can be as nerve racking as any accompanying human gestation.

Every writer must have help. In my case there has been a host of contributors beginning with parents, followed by gossipers I heard in filling stations or grocery stores during my boyhood in northern Indiana, teachers at all levels, wartime companions, and fellow faculty members at various universities.

I'm indebted to grammar teachers like Miss Donnelly in the second grade and university colleagues such as Keith Huntress and Clarence Matterson. Fellow members of an informal book club unknowingly made contributions, and close friends like Terry Schlunz followed my prose from its onset. Furthermore, I owe a great deal my publisher, Bob Babcock owner and chief executive of Deeds Publishing. There also was help from my granddaughter Caitlin Mills and tender memories of my deceased daughter Sandy. Dr. Ken Mills led me through computer mires as well as other puzzles.

My greatest debt is to my daughter Susan Mills, an eagle-eyed editor able to spot awkward syntax quicker than a robin can see the head of a worm emerging from its hole.

To Sue and others I give my thanks.

—Robert Underhill

ABOUT THE AUTHOR

Robert Underhill was born in Indiana, went through elementary and high schools in that state, and received his Bachelor's Degree in English from Manchester College. An Air Corps officer in both WWII and the Korean War, he was shot down over Poland during WWII while on his 50th mission and escaped the Nazis with the help of the Polish Underground.

Dr. Underhill earned his M.S. and Ph.D. from Northwestern University in Evanston, Illinois. After a brief stint of teaching at Northwestern, he accepted a position at Iowa State University in Ames, where he remained on the faculty as a classroom teacher or departmental administrator until his retirement as a professor emeritus of English and Speech.

In addition to scholarly articles, Underhill has written over twenty books, including biographies, novels, collections of essays, and both military and political histories.

CPSIA information can be obtained
at www.ICGtesting.com
Printed in the USA
FSHW021146080720
71569FS